Speaking Magic

To Vincent & Orlwen
& the love of performance

Carolyn Dickson

Oakhill Press

Akron & New York

Speaking Magic

Performance Strategies for
Winning Your Business Audience

by Carolyn Dickson
with Paula DePasquale

Speaking Magic

Library of Congress Cataloging-in-Publication Data

Dickson, Carolyn
  Speaking Magic : performance strategies for winning your business audience/ by Carolyn Dickson with Paula DePasquale.

  ISBN 0-9619590-8-8 (pb) : $12.95
  1. Business communication. 2. Oral communication. 3. Public speaking. I. DePasquale, Paula. II. Title.

HF5718.D574   1994
658.4'52 —dc20   94-
28384

          CIP

0 9 8 7 6 5 4 3

Third Printing, January 1996

I

The Magic of Performance

1

Making Magic Happen

*If all my possessions were taken from me with
one exception, I would choose to keep the power for
speech, for by it I would regain all the rest.*
—Daniel Webster

Imagine this. You're called to the podium...you start to speak...
and something wonderful happens. You feel dynamic and alive, and
your words flow without effort. Before you know it, your audience is
in the palm of your hand. Your presentation proclaims that you can
do the job. Your pitch turns into a sale. Your remarks become motivational highlights. It's obvious to everyone that you're a real pro.
And your audience responds to your power with understanding and
acceptance.

Sounds wonderful, doesn't it? Professionals in all the performance
arts—actors, dancers, musicians, athletes—speak about those moments when all the years of training fall into place and everything
"clicks." Time is suspended as performer and audience draw strength
from each other in an electric, emotion-charged connection. The best
performers experience this connection time and time again because
they've trained themselves so well that at performance time, it simply "happens."

As a speaker, you too are a performer. Not only are you the star of
the performance, you're also the writer, director, producer, and
choreographer of your drama. You're in charge of makeup, wardrobe, props, and lighting. Though your goals may be pragmatic and
concrete—to influence company policy, to shape budgets, to get the
job—like other performers you're also in the business of winning an
audience.

Unfortunately, most business speakers assume this level of excellence is beyond their reach. It isn't. Like all pros, you can train your-

self to make it happen. Studies consistently show that in business, communication skills top the list of qualities considered important for success. How well you communicate determines whether you and your ideas are accepted, whether you win the contract, keep the client, get the job, or walk away thinking "I've blown it." In fact, your speaking ability is not only the deciding factor in whether or not people listen to you, *it's an absolute requirement for leadership.*

Look around you and you'll see that the people who are the most successful are usually the best communicators, able to convey information in a way that touches other people personally. They can sell their ideas at all levels, within the organization and outside it. Some of these people have a natural flair for guiding, persuading, and influencing the people around them, while others have worked long and hard to acquire this talent.

As founder and president of VOICE-PRO Incorporated, I've spent years teaching business people and other professionals to improve their presentation skills by using many of the same techniques practiced in other areas of the performing arts. The tips, techniques, and exercises found here come from a variety of disciplines, including dance, theatre, sports, singing, and the martial arts. With them, you'll be able to overcome stagefright, relax under pressure, speak with power and authority, rehearse more effectively, and ultimately develop that elusive quality known as stage presence. Whether you're new to the presentation arena or just need a bit of polishing, you can use the information in this book to perfect your skills and become a more dynamic, exciting, and influential speaker.

The Gift of Speech

There seems to be a belief that you're either born a gifted speaker or you're not. Perhaps that's because the best speakers make it look so easy. But when asked their secret, these individuals invariably reply that this "gift" is something they've worked long and hard to acquire. Of course, it is true that some people are more outgoing than others, and sometimes this trait helps them to be better speakers. But not always. Extroverts may never be at a loss for words, but they're as likely as anyone else to suffer from stagefright or have trouble getting their point across.

So it's not unusual for men and women in business to find speaking before a group more difficult than they would like. An engineer once told me: "I'm a thing person, not a people person. I'd rather let someone else do the talking." He didn't see that he could be both, and that he was limiting his potential by focusing solely on his technical abilities. When he made presentations, he played it safe, falling back on corporate cliches and taking care not to be too conspicuous. In short, he aimed for mediocrity—and hit it on the nose.

Few people have ever received any real training in speaking and presentation. It's assumed that managers and executives should have some degree of speaking proficiency because their expertise in their own fields is expected to carry over into everything else they do. But when asked to give a luncheon address or an important presentation that could win a promotion or a new customer, these same "experts" become intimidated. Why? Simply because they lack the specialized skills they need to get their message across. Even those who have taken courses in speech communications find that often these classes focus on theory, not on practical skills.

An accountant friend sat across the lunch table from me and discussed the problem from his point of view. "We hire a young person," he said, "give him a desk in a corner and some work to do. If he does that work well, we give him a little more money, a bigger desk, and more difficult work. If he's good, pretty soon he has a cubbyhole of his own, with maybe a title, and his assignments get pretty sophisticated. This goes on for years. One day, because he's good at his work, stays in his cubbyhole and produces like crazy, he becomes a partner. And then we say, 'Now go out into the world and talk to people. Get involved in civic activities, have more client contact, and *bring in business!!!*' Has he had any training to help him succeed? No. Is he comfortable in his new role? No. Do we expect him to succeed anyway? We sure do."

How Do You Rate?

As human beings, we naturally communicate, whether we intend to or not. Watch any two-year-old for just a few minutes and you'll easily recognize whether she is hungry, happy, sleepy, or hurt. The most effective speakers build on their communicative instincts, hone their innate abilities and then develop the specific skills that get results in a business environment. In fact, without even realizing it, you may already have many of the qualities of a dynamic and exciting performer.

As you read through the following questions, let them help you assess the strengths and weaknesses you bring with you to the podium. Use this book to unlock your natural potential and develop to the fullest your abilities to reach and hold an audience.

What do you think about when you speak?
- Is your attention directed to the needs of your audience?
- Do your thoughts wander to your own success and well-being?
- Do you keep wondering, "How am I doing?"
- Do you look at your audience and see them as human beings?
- Do you watch for audience feedback and address both the positive and the negative without flinching?

How do you feel when you speak?
- Do you try to hide feelings of nervousness?
- Are your muscles loose and easy?
- Is your breathing deep and even, or do you often feel short of breath?
- Do you feel the free flow of energy through your body, or are you blocked with tension?
- Do you ever shut out the world and just "go through the motions"?
- Do you feel commitment to your message, and are you willing to let that commitment show?

How do you sound when you speak?
- Does your voice carry to the back of the room?
- Is your voice strong and pleasing, or is it hoarse, breathy, weak, or grating?
- Can your words be clearly understood?
- Is your voice filled with expression or do you speak in a monotone?
- Do you search for the best words to communicate your ideas?

How do you look when you speak?
- Do you "hold still" or are you able to move about comfortably?
- Do your gestures reinforce what you're saying?
- Are you ever concerned that your body will "betray" you?
- Does your appearance express your confidence in "who you are"?
- Do you feel genuine respect for your audience, or fear?

Do you take the time to prepare thoroughly, or do you generally "wing it"?

- Do your presentations have a beginning, a middle, and an end?
- Do your facts and figures clearly back up your main points?
- Do you read from a manuscript or speak from an outline?
- Do you know when and how to use microphones, lecterns, and visual aids?
- Can you recover from a blunder?
- Can you think on your feet and formulate an articulate response to a question?
- Are you persuasive? Do you inspire your listeners to action?

Connecting With Your Audience

The goal of every good speaker is to establish a connection with the audience, a bridge of shared understanding that links you together. All of a sudden, you're in tune, drawn to each other in an unspoken, yet powerful and emotional way.

In sports, the connection happens when athlete and crowd share the thrill of a great play. In the theatre, the play comes alive when both players and audience put aside their personal concerns and lose themselves in the actions and emotions of the characters. This comes about because of intense concentration and mental focus in both athlete and actor, which we'll look at closely in the next chapter.

In the meantime, you'll know you've made the connection when you look at the audience and know without a doubt that they're yours.

Becoming a performer who can connect with an audience requires risk-taking. In any discipline, it takes courage to realize your full potential. But it can be done. When you've succeeded and the connection is made, magic happens. The audience wins and so do you.

2

Focus: The First Step

Most professionals have days when they perform beyond expectations, but top performers in any field are able to perform at a consistently high level of expertise. They seem always to be "on."

Psychologist Abraham Maslow, who spent a lifetime studying what he termed "peak performance" experiences, found that at these times his subjects felt more confident and more mentally and physically integrated. They were "totally tuned in to the moment." Somehow, these feelings helped them perform in ways that far exceeded their expectations.

Certain mental characteristics are present in athletes during peak performance, according to Charles A. Garfield, author of *Peak Performance, Mental Training Techniques of the World's Greatest Athletes* (Warner Books, 1984). The athletes fully expect to succeed. They operate on automatic pilot and all their actions are spontaneous. Their concentration is intense, they become immersed in the activity, and they experience feelings of power and exhilaration. The performance state of these top athletes is characterized by very high energy coupled with a profound sense of inner calm.

When you're in a relaxed, resourceful state, you're able to do everything better. We've all had days when it seemed we could do no wrong, while at other times we've felt "off" and nothing we touched turned out right. What's the difference? Often it's the state we're in.

A state is the result of all the many physiological and neurological processes that are going on inside us. Some states, like the one that delivers peak performance, are enabling, while others leave us feeling paralyzed. Top performers understand and learn to control how they think and feel, using this knowledge to put themselves into an enabling performance state.

The key to achieving this ideal performance state is mental focus. It's the starting point for the building of any skill, and speaking skills are no exception. You will become the best speaker you can be when you develop the mental characteristics of other peak performers. To develop the mental toughness you need, you must forget about yourself and concentrate on serving the needs of your audience.

Discovering Mental Focus

What do you think about when you speak? Most people are focused on themselves and how they are being perceived by others. Your inner monologue during a presentation may go something like this: "My God, there are a lot of people here and they're all looking at me. I hope I can get through this without screwing up. What if I forget what I'm supposed to say? Or lose my place? OK, I'll just pretend they're not really here. The faster I talk, the sooner it will be over. I know they can tell I'm nervous. Uh oh, that really sounded stupid. Damn! I was afraid this would happen. If I can just get through this without making a complete fool of myself, I'll be satisfied."

If this sounds like you, notice that with every word you're focusing your thoughts directly onto yourself, with your own comfort and success becoming your primary concerns. If, however, you ignore the most important element in the presentation—your audience—you're making a big mistake. Adjusting your mental focus means putting aside your own personal agenda in order to meet the needs of that audience.

Audiences Are People, Too

For many of us, just the word "audience" is intimidating. If you take a moment to think about what "audience" means to you, you might be surprised at the images that come to mind.

One of my clients noticed that for her the word audience brought to mind rows of black-robed, stern judges about to pronounce her guilty of some unnamed crime. Another imagined a more unruly group, coughing, shuffling and whispering among themselves, while he desperately tried to win them over. Many speakers perceive the audience as a vast sea of empty faces.

Our mental images have a powerful impact on our emotions. So if pictures like these are flashing through your mind, you'll end up wanting to hide from your audience instead of trying to connect with them.

It helps to understand that audiences are people too. Whether you're speaking to the higher-ups in your organization or to the guys in the shop, your listeners are just a group of ordinary individuals who are motivated by the same personal and professional needs as you, and they're listening to you for one reason only—to have those needs met. So put yourself in their place. Instead of trying to impress them, or worrying about your own fate, ask yourself questions like:

- Why are these people here? What's in this for them?
- How can I make their jobs easier, their day brighter, or their lives better?
- How can I make this easy for them to understand?
- How do they want to be treated?

A sales manager described the power she felt when she realized for the first time that audiences are simply groups of people like herself. Betty had always felt confident and relaxed in one-on-one conversations, yet when she was in front of a group, nervousness often caused her to freeze. "Until now, it never occurred to me to treat an audience the same as I treat real people," she said. Once she was able to do that, her nervousness disappeared.

For me, this realization occurred one evening in the midst of a dinner speech. I looked out into the audience and, in mid-sentence, it hit me, "These people are thinking about themselves. They really don't care about me at all!" It was a wonderfully liberating moment, as I finally understood that, since they weren't thinking about me, I didn't have to think about me either. All I needed to do was speak directly and personally to their concerns. This insight into the "audience mind" makes speaking in any situation so much easier.

Focus Through Eye Contact

Many speakers believe that eye contact is something they should "do." But if your focus is on your audience where it belongs, you will quite naturally look at them. A complacent young man once described the method he used to "relate" to his audience: "I pick a spot on the back wall about six inches above their heads, and I look at that spot while I'm talking. They all think I'm making eye contact, and I don't have to look at them at all. I really have them fooled." Other speakers lock their eyes onto those of an audience member while they count to three, or to four, or to five, and then robotlike move on to someone else.

In these cases, the real reason for looking at people has been forgotten. The goal, remember, is connection with the audience. The purpose of making eye contact is to establish an emotional tie between you. By letting the audience see into your eyes, you give them a glimpse of a real person; and by watching them carefully, you receive important feedback about what they're thinking and feeling.

Focusing on the audience means *looking* at them. Not through them, or past them, or over their heads to a spot on the wall. (You pick it up immediately when someone does that to you, and so will your listeners.) When you see a gleam of understanding in someone's eye, you know you're being heard. If you spot a raised eyebrow or a quizzical look, you can deal with it on the spot. How do you know they're with you? If you're really looking, you'll pick up the signals. Incidentally, you'll receive an added benefit because, if you're this actively involved with the audience, you're much too busy to create frightening or distorted images of them in your mind.

You'll notice that I haven't asked you to imagine the audience naked, or to visualize them as little people three feet tall, or to use any other kind of trick intended to make you feel instantly superior to them. That's because I've seen that kind of advice backfire over and over again. When you demean other people, you demean yourself. On the other hand, connection happens when real human beings relate to each other in an honest, human way.

Letting Go Of Ego

Adjusting your mental focus also means letting go of your ego, or more specifically your ego thoughts. Ego thoughts are primarily concerned with self. They subject us to harassment from what I call our "inner judges," those tormenting voices that well up from deep down inside us because we tend to be our own worst critics. Preoccupation with these inner judges is the number one cause of the emotional stress we call stagefright.

With ego thoughts, the key words of your inner monologue are *I* and *me*. Often, ego thoughts take the form of questions such as: How am I doing? Do I look nervous? Will I make the sale? What will my boss think? Am I winning or losing?

With audience thoughts, the key words are *they* and *them*. What are *they* looking for? How can I make this easy for *them?* When your mind is occupied with audience thoughts, you'll discover that, without even trying, you watch them more carefully and become aware of their reactions sooner. You'll also find yourself using language that makes sense to them and touches on their special areas of concern.

As the president of Voice-Pro, I spend a lot of time making presentations to many different audiences. How well I do can have a direct impact on the success of the business, so I often feel under pressure to give a flawless performance. In typical Carolyn fashion, I find myself beset by doubts. When I tune in to my own inner monologue, it sounds much like the one I described earlier.

"OK, Carolyn," I find my inner judges saying, "you're supposed to be the expert, so you'd better be good. If you make a mistake, you'll look stupid, so be careful. If you're not perfect, they won't like you, so be careful. If you aren't the best speaker they've ever heard, your business will suffer. So be careful, be careful, be careful."

If I let these destructive thoughts continue for very long I find that I'm afraid...afraid of losing credibility...afraid to take risks...afraid I will fail. When this happens, I have a job to do. Before I can step out on the stage and speak to any audience, I must silence my inner judges. So I have a conversation with them. I tell them that I understand what they're doing and that in their own way they're trying to keep me safe from criticism and failure. But right now I'm busy and I want them to go away. I simply haven't the time to worry about making mistakes.

Then I consciously and deliberately shift the focus of my attention to my audience. I tell myself that these are regular people who aren't the least bit interested in my fears. And that the well-being of my business isn't their concern. All they want is for me to give them something that can help them become better at what they do. My job isn't to satisfy me; it's to satisfy *them*.

Winning Through Focus

When you change your inner monologue to reflect the needs of the audience, you're managing your mental focus and staying in command of your thoughts. And in so doing, you'll be able to keep your speaking situation in perspective.

It's true that some of your presentations are more important to you professionally than others. In the same way that the quality of my speaking has a direct bearing on my business, an impressive performance on your part may win you a raise, a promotion, or an exciting new assignment; blundering through could be a major embarrassment. But if you let your preoccupation with these eventualities override your concerns for the audience, you put overwhelming pressure on yourself and severely limit your chances for success.

Like peak performing athletes and entertainers, top business speakers are "totally tuned in to the moment." They're immersed in what's going on right now, with the past forgotten and the future dismissed as unimportant. No matter how much you need the customer's signature on the dotted line or how badly you want the new vice presidency, when you're making your presentation, you must believe these issues don't matter. They're out of your control and you can't afford to worry about them.

Instead, take charge of the variables you can control, and mental focus is the place to start. Think about what's in it for the audience. Create an inner monologue that takes them into account. Look at them, see them as human beings, and talk to them like real people. You'll notice an immediate improvement in your level of performance, and you'll be able to put your inner judges to rest, once and for all.

The essential message of this chapter is that the audience is worthy of your loving care and attention. The message of the next chapter is that so are you.

3

The Message and You

A city that is set on a hill cannot be hid. Neither do men light a candle and put it under a bushel, but on a candlestick; and it giveth light unto all that are in the house. Let your light so shine before men, that they may see your good works.
—Matthew 5:14
King James Bible

Studies of the way audiences assimilate information show that the content of a presentation—the words themselves—accounts for about seven percent of what your audiences will actually receive and process. Thirty-eight percent of the message is received in the way it sounds (that's your voice and how you use it). And a whopping fifty-five percent is carried visually, in your face, hands, and body. Fully ninety-three percent of your message then, is experienced by your audience in the way you deliver it.

Researchers have found that words produce a characteristic electrical pattern in the brain. A particular brain wave pattern occurs when you think about or say the word "anger," for example, and the same patterns appear to hold true from person to person, even in people who speak different languages. When programmed to recognize these brain wave patterns, computers can tell you what word you're thinking even before you speak it.

What's the significance? This research indicates that at the most basic human level—that of your brain wave patterns—the words you speak have both a physical and emotional effect on you. When you speak about anger, or hope, or fear, or success, or honor, certain neurological changes take place in your body. You and your words are joined together, inseparable from each other.

Not only then, are you the medium through which your message flows, you actually become the message. The audience doesn't differentiate between who you are, what you say, and how you say it. To the audience, you and the message are one. Your words indefinably change because you utter them. Your presentations are unique because you as a human being are unique. If you doubt the importance of the performer to the performance, just think about the difference between reading a play and experiencing live theatre...or looking at a printed score and sitting in a concert hall hearing the same music played by a symphony orchestra.

The Importance of You

Human beings are social animals. We need the stimulation, the caring, the connection that we get from our contacts with other people almost as much as we need the food we eat.

One of the trends that John Naisbitt identified in his book, *Megatrends* (Warner Books, 1982), is an increasing need for connectedness. Naisbitt theorized that as the use of technology in our society increases, isolation also increases, causing people to feel an even greater need to experience personal interaction. He calls this phenomenon "high-tech/high touch."

A writer friend laughingly drove this point home to me when she told about using her new computer for the first time. She had spent long, lonely hours editing a manuscript and was finally satisfied with her efforts. Tired but happy, she attempted to save her material, inadvertently pressed the wrong key and poof! Her work was gone. Sputtering with frustration, she dialed the phone to call me and got...my recorded voice message.

The CEO of a large Cleveland advertising agency seems to intuitively understand the importance of personal interaction when it comes to recognizing and motivating people. George has a brass bell mounted in the office lobby. When a new account is won, the clanging bell summons the staff to the conference room for a festive announcement and a toast. While time and money could be saved by making the announcement by inter-office memo, it wouldn't be nearly as much fun or as rewarding for the people involved.

We are bombarded today by information and surrounded by technology. That's why, more than ever, audiences need live speakers—not so they can get the facts delivered up with mechanical perfection, but so they can feel connected with another human being. Yes, they want and need the information you have for them, but they also want to get your interpretation of that information, to feel your presence, and to experience the power of your personality.

The Impact of Self-Esteem

How you feel about yourself has a tremendous impact on the way you and your message are received by others. The term "self-esteem" is used to excess these days, and it sometimes seems as if poor self-esteem is being blamed for almost every personal problem and social ill of our time. But perhaps that's not surprising, since self-esteem does have a profound effect on one's thoughts, emotions, words, actions, and interactions with others. When you know who you are, where you stand, what's important to you, and why your opinion is of value, the force of your personality and your message will have a greater impact on your audience.

Self-esteem has two components, self-respect and confidence. This means that it stems from the conviction that you're both worthy and competent. Ideally, your self-respect is unaffected by the opinions of others and remains unchanged regardless of their approval or disapproval. You know that no matter how you struggle, you are worthy—simply because you exist. This concept seems so simple, but for many of us, learning to accept the truth of it is the achievement of a lifetime.

As a person with self-respect, and as a speaker, you have a right to the considerate attention of others, your words are as valuable as those of anyone else, and the disapproval of others cannot diminish your worth as a person. For these reasons, when you speak, you cannot lose.

Unlike self-respect, which is inherent, self-confidence is situation based. It's gained over time through preparation and experience. Self-confidence is the assurance that you have the knowledge and skill necessary to get the job done. A trial lawyer of twenty years once told me, "Nothing surprises me anymore. I've seen it all before, and I know that, no matter what they throw at me, I'll be able to handle it." His unshakable confidence is a result of long years of experience.

A few years ago, I enrolled in a wilderness program at the Colorado Outward Bound School in the Rocky Mountains. During this program, my greatest challenge was The Rock, the sheared face of a cliff ninety feet straight up. With harness securely in place, I was told to start climbing. So I climbed. Or rather I crawled, scraped, and inched my way up the face of that awful rock. Afflicted with "sewing machine leg," the violent shaking of knees so dreaded by climbers, I struggled to find tiny outcroppings of rock that would take my quivering weight; and the tips of my fingers left bloody little marks on the granite face. For what seemed like hours I was stuck in one place, with only the calls of encouragement from friends on the ground to keep me from dropping back and admitting defeat.

Finally, with tears streaming down my face, I made it to the top. I—wife, mother, grandmother, singer, speaker, businesswoman, ordinary person—had triumphed. I had done the impossible. I had climbed *The Rock.*

This event had a great impact on my self-esteem. It took courage to overcome my fear of climbing, courage I didn't know I had. Because I've proven that I have the required skills to climb that rock, I'm confident that I could do it again. My self-respect also improved as a result of that climb, and because self-respect is open-ended, it continues to grow and influence all other aspects of my life, including my speaking and teaching.

You don't need to climb a mountain in Colorado or have twenty years of experience trying court cases to develop the self-esteem you need to feel comfortable interacting with an audience. As a human being, you are worthy to be a speaker. You are special, you have something to say, and you deserve to be heard. These are facts to which there can be no argument. Then as you build your speaking skills and gain experience in the presentation arena, your confidence in your abilities will grow. You'll know that you can win the attention of your audience, keep them interested in what you have to say, and motivate them to action because you've done it before. Even if the slide projector explodes or you're placed in the worst possible time slot on the program.

Individuality Is Power

It seems there is an unspoken rule in many companies that all presentations must be cut from the same mold, delivered up in the same "just the facts ma'am" style. No wonder so many speakers are boring. But you don't have to bore your audiences to death. You bring something of immense value to your presentation—your intelligence, your warmth, your own personal style. If you let it, your personality can make all the difference.

Many young professionals come through our courses, sent by their companies to gain polish. We often find that, while they tell themselves they're in class to improve their speaking skills, what they're really trying to do is act older. But youth isn't easily hidden, and in their attempts to be mature, they disappear behind a facade that is superficial and dull. As we work with these young people, they begin to develop the easy assurance of manner that comes from poise. They discover that they don't have to fake it and that all their personal qualities—their youth, their intelligence, and their own individual talents—are an asset.

The point is that individuality is power. When you are free to be yourself...to be young or old...tall or short...male or female...introverted or extroverted...you gain extraordinary power. The dynamic spark of your personality brings your words to life. And your audience, no matter what mold they might have expected you to fit into, will respond to your personal power by paying you the highest of compliments. They will listen.

You have great strengths—don't hide them. If you have a quick wit, or an analytical mind, or a strong sense of purpose, or whatever unique trait sets you apart from other people, let it show. It puzzles me to see how many speakers shut down their personalities when they face an audience, negating their own strengths as they try to behave like someone else. How much better to be openly, honestly willing to let the real you stand up and be heard.

The Audience Paradox

Speaking before groups is a joint venture. Speaker and audience need each other. Facts and figures, no matter how impressive, aren't enough. The audience paradox starts with the concept that serving the needs of your audience is the only thing that matters when you speak. But you can accomplish this only when you feel strong inside and confident of your abilities to give the speech you want to give. Then, and only then, will you feel free to be yourself.

When you are comfortable in your own skin, when you are willing to "become the message," the power of your personality will give your presentation strength, conviction, warmth, and presence. Your presentation will work because of you.

II

Relaxation Magic

4

Releasing Physical Tension

Stagefright is like the character in "The Turn of the Screw" who never appears: he is always waiting outside the door, any door, waiting to get you. You either battle or walk away.
—Laurence Olivier

Stagefright knows no bounds. At one time or another it strikes almost everyone, ranging all the way from a mild case of jitters to feelings of abject terror. At the beginning of each of our classes, we ask the participants what they want most to gain from the upcoming training. Nearly everyone says something about wanting to feel more comfortable when speaking before a group. Of all the qualities a good speaker can possess, the most prized is the ability to relax under the pressure of performance.

This chapter, and the two that follow, are about relaxation. In them you'll find the skills you need to keep yourself calm under fire, skills that will become the core of your overall performance technique. And you'll learn that the best way to speak is the easy way— free of physical tension, cool-headed, self-possessed, and mentally clear.

Performance anxiety is in part a mental state, as you learned in Chapter 2 when you examined the mischief your ego thoughts and inner judges can cause. That's why the technique of adjusting mental focus is an important piece of the relaxation puzzle.

But stagefright also can produce physical symptoms in performers. The clammy hands, pounding heart, breathlessness, nervous stomach, and shaky muscles that so many people experience aren't imaginary. They're very real indeed. You can't just tell yourself to relax. You need to know something about how your body works

under stress. Once you know that, you can learn what to do about
the butterflies, the shortness of breath, and the quivering knees.

The Flight or Fight Response

Any threat, whether it's real or you only imagine it, can trigger
the flight or fight response, which is your body's natural reaction to
the perception of danger. The instant you feel threatened, your sym-
pathetic nervous system surges into action, releasing the hormone
epinephrine (commonly called adrenalin), and two other hormones,
norepinephrine (also called noradrenalin), and dopamine. The
onslaught of these three hormones brings about complex and powerful changes in your body.

The action of your heart increases, and you may feel it beating
faster as it works to pump more blood per minute. In order to use the
blood supply more efficiently, your blood vessels constrict, virtually
shutting down organs not essential for running or fighting. This is
the reason your stomach may feel queasy, as blood is redirected from
the gastrointestinal tract to your heart and skeletal muscles.

In your lungs, the bronchial tubes expand and you breathe
faster. You may even feel out-of-breath as your body strives to take
in more air. Salivary secretion declines, often resulting in a dry
mouth, and perspiration increases. All over your body, your muscles
tighten. In earlier times, extreme muscle tension made it more difficult for the spears of rival tribesmen to cause serious injury. And
although your rivals don't throw real spears today, you may still feel
the same tightening when you face a formidable opponent at the
negotiation table or look out over the podium at 150 sales managers
from the West Coast.

Reacting to "Flight or Fight"

Even though you're not in real physical danger, the flight or fight
response can play havoc with your reactions to the challenges of a
speaking situation. The adrenalin rush and the physical symptoms it
produces can throw you off balance. "I didn't expect to be this nervous," you think, as you try to control your pounding heart and
sweaty palms, hoping that no one else will notice. Now, with the
worry about being nervous piled on top of all the other concerns you
have about your presentation, you're in the throes of a "fear-pro-
duces nervousness-produces more fear" chain reaction. You need to

relax and adjust your mental focus in order to break the pattern and bring it to a halt.

The best performers are those who can channel the adrenalin rush to their advantage. They welcome the flight or fight response because they know it gives them an explosion of energy that will get them "up" for the occasion. At the same time they are able to stay calm and composed under the most stressful circumstances because they take the physical sensations they experience in their stride. Unfortunately, less skilled speakers react to this hormonal hodge-podge by disintegrating into quivering wrecks, or going into a state I call "overcontrol."

Sondra was a typical quivering wreck. When her nervousness took over, she was unable to stand still, so she paced restlessly in front of the audience. Because she was afraid to look at people, her eyes darted about the room and her chin jerked up and to the right with the beginning of each sentence. Her speech was permeated with fillers—ah's and uh's everywhere—along with frequent nervous giggles. Her voice shook and she had trouble catching her breath. Whenever Sondra spoke, it was evident to everyone that she was scared to death.

Overcontrol, on the other hand, is characterized by a rigid, overly passive manner. You see it in the speaker who has a "great stone face" and a monotone voice. Sam was the dynamic, innovative CEO of a turnaround company. He had, almost by the force of his personality alone, rebuilt his organization from the ground up. Yet when Sam spoke to professional groups about his accomplishments, there was no indication of his abundant personal power. He shut off his personality, read from a prepared script, and carefully controlled his every movement so that he could avoid even the tiniest mistake. Sam successfully hid the nervousness he felt, but in doing so he bored his audience to death.

Scanning For Trouble Spots

When you understand your body's signals and know how to handle them, you won't have to suffer from overcontrol or turn into a quivering wreck. You can relax at will, loosening tense muscles and using the released energy to spark your presentations. In order to do this, you need to recognize your "trouble spots," those personal hiding places where you store excess tension. Common trouble spots are the jaw, the back of the neck, the shoulders, and the knees.

If any of your joints or muscles ache at the end of a particularly stress-filled day, your body is giving you a clear indication of where to find your trouble spots. If the messages are more subtle and you aren't quite sure where your trouble spots lie, the technique of body scanning will help you identify them and ease away hidden tension. Try this now.

Body Scanning

1. Sit comfortably with your feet on the floor. Close your eyes and breathe easily.
2. Turn your attention to your feet. Are they resting easily on the floor? Do you feel any tension in your feet? If you do, let it slip away.
3. Now turn your attention to your ankles, then your knees, then hips. In each area, check for unwanted tension and release it. Let it go.
4. Move through your entire body, checking for tension in your abdomen and lower back, waist, upper back, shoulders, arms, hands, and fingers.
5. Release the tension in your neck, jaw, and forehead.
6. When you have completed the mental passage through your body, take a breath and, as you release it, give up your weight to the chair. Let the chair support you as you sit, weightless, for a few moments.
7. When you have completed your body scan, open your eyes and read on.

Body scanning requires you to use your inner awareness to pinpoint and relax areas of tension, which makes it a great way to practice mental focus. You're consciously directing your thoughts along predetermined pathways and instructing your body to react in specified ways. At first, scanning requires a little time and effort, but with practice it can be done quickly and almost automatically. You can scan anywhere, standing in a bank line, driving in traffic, or sitting in a meeting. And scanning before a presentation will calm you down and help to clear your mind for the performance ahead.

Reducing Physical Tension

Physical tension is blocked energy. The flight or fight response provides you with a wonderful, and very useful, rush of energy. But when your muscles are blocked with tension, you can't take advantage of it. So the unused energy builds, the block gets bigger, and you feel more and more uptight.

Professional athletes know the importance of releasing this kind of tension before an event. How do they do it? They move. A batter at the plate, a swimmer on the starting block, a sprinter waiting for the starting gun—all "shake out" to release the energy stored in their muscles. The Shrug and the Shake are simple exercises designed to help you do the same thing.

The Shrug

1. Stand with your feet shoulder-width apart and parallel. to each other. Relax your knees so they're not locked.
2. Raise your right shoulder up to your ear, then let it drop. (Don't cheat by lowering your ear to your shoulder.) The trick is to loosen your muscles so the shoulder drops of its own accord. Feel the release and the little bounce as it hits bottom.
3. Raise and drop your right shoulder three more times, then repeat with the left one. Again, release your muscles and let gravity take the weight of your arm.
4. Now lift both shoulders and let them fall. Repeat four times. Get a sense of your shoulders in their lowered position. They should feel easy and slightly heavy.
5. When your shoulders feel relaxed, let your arms hang at your sides with hands dangling. Check for tension in your arms and gently shake it loose.

The Shake

1. Stand with your feet shoulder-width apart and parallel to each other. Begin to wiggle your fingers—just your fingers.
2. Now add your hands and shake them too. Add, one by one, your elbows, shoulders, chest, waist, hips, knees, and feet, until you are shaking all over.
3. Let your head move with your body and add your voice to the action, shaking all the way down to your toes.
4. Come slowly to a stop and let yourself settle. Check your shoulders to make sure they're still loose. Then breathe easily and deeply, down into your body.

If you feel a little silly experimenting with these exercises, remember that you won't be shaking out while you're in front of your peers or with the board of directors looking on. This practice can take place at home, in your office with the door closed, or in any other private place. With daily repetition, your muscles will learn to respond immediately to your call for relaxation. Before a presentation, you can duck into the restroom or close your office door, do a few Shrugs and Shakes, and you'll be ready to go. You'll find that releasing pent-up tension puts you in command of yourself and frees you up for easy, coordinated movement.

Breathing to Relax

The best way of all to relax your body and focus your mind is simply to breathe. Diaphragmatic, or deep breathing, is the oldest and still the most effective stress-reducing technique known. It's been used for thousands of years to quell anxiety and promote a generalized state of well-being. Hatha Yoga is built on various patterns of breathing, as are many of the martial arts such as T'ai Chi and Kung Fu. Breathing has even been proven to be an effective pain reducing technique, which is why it's taught in natural childbirth classes.

Many people think that deep breathing means taking great big gulps of air, but the word "deep" actually refers to positioning in the body. Breathing is deep when air is pulled into the lower third of the lungs by the action of the diaphragm, or breathing muscle. When you breathe diaphragmatically, expansion and contraction occur in your midsection, allowing your chest and shoulders to remain quiet. Watch a sleeping child and you'll notice his belly rises and falls—body relaxed, diaphragm working. Deep breathing is the natural way to breathe.

Deep breathing is less fatiguing than thoracic (or upper chest) breathing because it uses less energy and allows more blood to be oxygenated with each breath. Body and mind are fueled to operate more efficiently. There is also research that indicates deep breathing quiets the mind through a neural mechanism that actually reduces brain activity.

Breathing exercises are among the first we ask our clients to do. They not only calm the jitters almost everyone feels at the beginning of one of our classes, but also provide a tool they can use as they prepare for presentations they give back on the job. Whenever I conduct breathing exercises, a lovely calm settles over the room and everyone in it. Clients report they are able to reproduce that calm within themselves just by going through these exercises.

The Hiss

1. Sit erect with your feet flat on the floor. Rest your arms in your lap or on the arms of your chair, and relax your shoulders.
2. Take a gentle breath—not too much. Then Hiss to the end of your breath, imagining that there is a hole in the small of your back just below your waist. Gently direct all the air and the sound of the Hiss down through your body and out that hole in your back. (The hiss will sound like an ordinary hiss. Only your mental image changes.)
3. When you feel empty, Hiss out a little more. Then let the air reenter your body as it left—from the bottom up.
4. Hiss several times, feeling yourself settle with each breath. See if you can locate the base of the Hiss, somewhere in your lower body.

Relaxing the Jaw

The jaw is a particular trouble spot for many people. Tension often accumulates in the temperomandibular joint (TMJ), the spot where the jaw connects with the skull. For obvious reasons, this joint is vitally important to the speaker. Tension here can result in clenched teeth, making a speaker appear angry. It can inhibit diction, projection, and clarity, and result in a "plastic," insincere looking smile.

The speaking problems that stem from a tight jaw can be alleviated by exercises that combine deep breathing and muscle relaxation.

The Ha's

1. Place your fingers in front of your earlobes, on the hinge where your jaw connects to your skull. Loosen the hinge and allow your jaw to drop open vertically as far as it will go without strain. When you feel your jaw fully open, you may bring your hands down.
2. With your jaw unhinged, say easily: Ha...Ha...Ha. After completing the exercise once, repeat the three Ha's, but this time send the air and sound of the Ha's down through your body and out the opening in the small of your back. (Just like the Hiss.)

3. Feel the depth of sound in your body. If your jaw tightens, loosen it up. If you feel any tension in your upper body, let it go.

The Blah's

1. Unhinge your jaw. Relaxing all the muscles in your face, say: Blah...Blah...Blah. Drop your jaw with each word. "Blah" means "nothing." Say the word according to its meaning. Let your face go slack.
2. Repeat the exercise, directing the air and sound down through your body and out the hole in your back. Feel the relaxation in your face, neck, and shoulders. Let your jaw drop vertically with each Blah.

The Blah's Plus Ten

1. Keeping the looseness in your face that you felt while saying Blah, count slowly to ten. Drop your jaw with each number. For the purposes of this exercise, it's OK to sacrifice diction in order to achieve the desired relaxation. You'll put it back later.
2. When you have experienced counting with complete facial relaxation, go back and count again, this time pronouncing each number clearly. The muscles of your face and jaw should remain loose and easy.

Let Your Energy Work For You

"Let your nervousness work for you," is a piece of advice often tossed about by people who don't really understand what it means. Your nervousness won't ever work for you, but your energy will. When stagefright hits, the flight or fight response generates an explosion of energy that is meant to be burned up in intense, physical activity. Normally, however, speaking doesn't demand the extreme exertion required for a fight, and when you're giving a financial report to the executive staff, you can't run away.

This is the beginning of the relaxation process. Focus, deep breathing, and the loosening of muscle tension unlock the energy that often disguises itself as performance anxiety. You'll learn to channel that energy in future chapters. But now let's give you a home base to work from.

5

Starting From Home Base

When I was six years old, my family moved to a new house, so along with the normal apprehension of starting first grade, I had the additional burden of being the new kid on the block. I have a vivid recollection of standing in a circle with my fellow pupils on that first day, while our teacher talked to us about good posture. Wanting desperately to belong, I stood rigidly at attention—head held high, spine swayed as I strained to keep my chest out and my shoulders back, with knees locked to hold me in place. Recognizing my eagerness, and intending to make me feel welcome, the teacher said, "Look at Carolyn. Isn't she standing up nice and straight!"

It was the kiss of death. I managed over time to perfect that rigidity until the threat of nodules on my vocal cords and a ruptured disk forced me to acknowledge that I had to loosen up if I wanted to save my career and my health. My "good" posture was practically killing me.

There are good reasons why dancers, actors, athletes, and musicians pay special attention to body position and skeletal alignment. When you're in balance, with your bones and muscles all in the right places doing what they're supposed to, you look good, sound good, and feel good. Your mind works more clearly and it's easy for you to move. As a speaker, you benefit from this in two ways.

First of all, your appearance shapes your message in all kinds of ways. Watch people on the street or in a waiting room or elevator. Notice how quickly you form opinions about them just by the way they carry themselves. Is he an executive or a ballplayer? Did she just make the sale or watch someone else walk away with it? Does this person have status, or not? You have very little real evidence to help you make your decisions, but that won't stop you. Using nothing but visual cues, you'll make almost instantaneous judgments about the people you're watching, judgments that will stay with you and won't be easy to change later.

To an audience, this makes a world of difference. You can send any message about yourself that you choose, simply by changing the configuration of your body. Authority and strength can be conveyed without saying a word; the way you carry yourself will tell the whole story. Strike a casual pose, and feel the message soften and change. If you sit like you have a poker up your back, you'll look rigid and unyielding; slumped shoulders will tell the world you feel insecure.

From your own point of view, the benefit is much more personal. Good posture is relaxing. You can never be completely tension-free when you're out of skeletal alignment, and you'll find that when you're standing and sitting correctly, you don't get as tired. I was erroneously taught to think of correct posture as "feet together, chest thrust out, tummy in, and shoulders pulled up and back," and a great many people tell me they received the same misinformation as children. We have all suffered as a result, because this is actually an unnatural and unhealthy stance. Not only that, it's terribly uncomfortable.

Understanding Good Posture

One way to understand good, healthy posture is to think of the three major weights of your body as blocks hung on a string. These three blocks are your head, chest, and pelvis. When they are aligned correctly, a string holding them together vertically will pass through the exact center of each block. Gravity keeps these weights balanced. When the blocks are aligned properly, your muscles don't have to work overtime to keep them in place.

The Thinking Body, by Mabel E. Todd, (Paul B. Hoeber, Inc., 1937) long considered the Bible for dancers and students of movement, says it this way: "Bones are for support; muscles are for movement." When muscles do the work of bones, pulling or holding your body out of line, strain and fatigue are the result. Locked into holding patterns, your muscles aren't available to do their real job, which is to move you easily from position to position.

John was sent to me by his boss. John was intelligent, well-educated, technically proficient, and had good management skills. John would have been on the fast track to corporate success, but for one problem. People thought he was arrogant. John seemed to "talk down" to people, intimidating subordinates and clients alike. "He's really not like that once you get to know him," his boss said. "I can't figure out what the problem is."

When John walked into class, it was apparent to me that his problem was his posture. He was indeed "talking down" to people, with his chin pushed sharply forward and his nose held high in the air. When John loosened the neck muscles that were holding his head out of line, his gaze leveled, his look softened, and he lost the arrogant manner that had been causing him so much trouble.

John confided later that, when he was a high school sophomore, his football coach instructed him to protect the back of his neck from injury by raising his shoulders and tipping his head back. Now, at thirty-seven years old and long past his football days, his career was in jeopardy because he was still walking around trying "to save his neck."

You may have succeeded in tuning out your parents and teachers when they told you to "Quit slouching and stand up straight," but it's time to examine how you stand, sit, and carry yourself now that you're an adult. Use body scanning to "listen" to your body. Do you feel your muscles "holding" anywhere? Are your head, chest, and pelvis out of line? Are you supporting your weight with muscle strength rather than skeletal alignment? If your answer to any of these questions is yes, you have some work to do.

Finding Home Base

Athletes in every sport learn a personal home base, a position from which they start and to which they return between plays. At the plate, the batter sets his feet, bends his knees, and positions his body so his swing will have optimum power. When you play tennis, the home base of knees bent, racket held waist high, and weight rolled lightly forward on the balls of your feet allows you to reach a ball anywhere on the court. Obviously you won't play two hours of tennis locked into this position, but you always come back to it between shots.

Musicians also learn to adopt a comfortable home base position early in their training. I once watched a group of tiny Suzuki violinists rehearse for a recital. One by one, these four-year-olds walked onto the stage, each carrying a large paper circle. Solemnly they placed their circles on the floor and positioned themselves so the outsides of their feet were just touching the edges of the paper. Carefully, painstakingly, they were building a home base that would last them a lifetime of performances. Then they straightened, looked at the audience for a moment, tucked their miniature instruments under their chins, and played like angels.

For the speaker, home base is called Neutral Position. It places you in correct skeletal alignment and provides you a place to start, a place to finish, and a place to return time and time again during a presentation. Clients often tell us that the concepts of home base and Neutral Position quickly become the most valuable aspects of their training.

Neutral Position I

1. Stand with your feet shoulder-width apart, six to ten inches. (If you want to be more precise, make yourself a paper circle.). Your feet should be parallel with toes pointed forward. Balance your weight equally over the balls and heels of your feet.

2. Check your knees to make sure they're not locked. They should be easy and springy, so you can move in any direction. Tilt your pelvis slightly forward.

3. Let your arms hang easily at your sides. If you are completely relaxed, your hands should hit your thighs slightly toward the front. You should actually feel your hands brush your thighs. (Some people have so much shoulder tension that their hands extend out stiffly with lots of space between hand and thigh.)

4. Do a couple of Shrugs and feel your shoulders settle into their lowered position. Imagine that you have a bucket of sand in each hand. Let the weight of the sand pull your shoulders down even further, then release the buckets and allow your shoulders to ease into a relaxed position.

5. Keep your chest open. Be careful not to round your shoulders or let them droop forward.

6. Float your head. The high point of your body is the crown of your head. Feel that you are suspended on a string from the ceiling. (It may help you to imagine helium balloons attached behind each ear, lifting your whole head gently upward.)

7. Standing easily in this Neutral Position, gently ease any tension that you may feel. Remember, bones are for support, muscles are for movement. Relax your muscles and hang in space.

Neutral Position is a natural stance that allows your energy to flow freely. It helps speakers get rid of the junk—the nervous mannerisms, the wiggles and twitches, and the restless drifting feet that are so distracting to an audience. Because it's free of tension, Neutral Position is also a powerful posture. If you're locked into faulty alignment or afflicted with nervous twitches, those weaknesses will be magnified by your lack of an effective home base to work from. But once you've become comfortable in neutral, you can change your message by shifting your weight, gesturing, and even moving around the stage without losing power.

Speakers who can stand quietly in neutral when they are counting sometimes find that the tension returns as soon as they try to make sense with their words. Neutral Position II adds the element of speech.

Neutral Position II

1. Stand in easy Neutral Position, with muscles relaxed.
2. Pick a spot on the opposite wall at eye level and focus your attention on that spot.
3. Count out loud to ten, feeling your breath and the sound of your voice settling deep in your body. Keep your eyes on the back wall.
4. As you count, feel yourself sink mentally into nothingness. Quietly notice any tension creeping into your muscles and ease it away. Pay particular attention to your jaw, shoulders, hands, and knees.
5. After you have counted to ten while remaining successfully in neutral, begin to speak. Introduce yourself to an imaginary group (keeping your eyes on the wall). If you have a real speech to give, practice it now—in neutral.
6. Any time you feel yourself losing the sense of neutral, stop and go back to counting. After a while you'll be able to shift in and out of Neutral Position without losing your train of thought.

Learning From Nature

When you perform, your feet belong on the floor, grounded firmly, while your upper body is fluid, with head, shoulders, and arms relaxed. But if you watch speakers carefully, you'll notice that many of them reverse this, holding their upper bodies tight for support while their lower bodies move restlessly. The speaker who paces back and forth with shoulders up, elbows pinned to his sides, and pointer clutched tightly in his hand is a good example. This results in rigidity and jerky, unnatural movements.

To put this in perspective and initiate any kind of physical change, we need to learn from nature. Trees are rooted in the ground with leaves and branches swaying gracefully in the wind. The foundation of a building is always at the bottom. Practitioners of T'ai Chi Chu'uan say: "Below the waist we are earth; above the waist we are water."

During the writing of this book, I went on a cross country ski holiday. After years of huffing and puffing and trying to keep up with my family, I decided that this was the time to learn the right way to ski once and for all. So I took some lessons. And guess what. I discovered that my same old postural problems had reared their ugly heads again. My back was arched, my shoulders were tight, my arms were too stiff, and I wasn't bending my knees enough (just like when I was six).

Then I learned that the fundamentals of the Nordic skier's home base are much the same as the speaker's Neutral Position—feet shoulder width apart, knees unlocked, shoulders down and relaxed with arms swinging freely, and head floated. The base of support for both skier and speaker is in the pelvis, not the shoulders. When I realized that the same postural principles applied, I was able to use speaking techniques to make an immediate improvement in my skiing. This may sound incredible, but the transfer of skills was easy since it was in accordance with natural law.

Power Begins With Stillness

As you experiment with Neutral Position, you'll find there is a big difference between "holding still" and being motionless. Holding still is tight and constricted, while motionless neutral is grounded, relaxed, and ready. From neutral you can move anywhere—across the platform, to the flipchart, or to sit on the edge of a table. Yet power begins with stillness. So when you want to be at your most powerful, come back to neutral and just stand there.

The components of a relaxed state now include focus, deep breathing, the release of muscular tension, the motionless comfort of Neutral Position, and operating from a strong, secure home base. The final piece of the puzzle will fall into place for you when you learn to center yourself.

6

Discovering Your Center

Like a great sea, peaceful on the surface, deep
and powerful within
—From the I Ching

The exercises for Neutral Position and home base outlined in the last chapter are difficult for many people because it's very hard to just do nothing. But power begins with stillness. If you can manage to quiet your mind and your body for even a little while, you will discover the source of your own personal power.

There's a spot somewhere deep inside you that is your center. It's the center of your posture, the center of your balance, the center of your breath, the center of your emotions. Knowing exactly where it is isn't as important as just knowing it is there. It is the core of you.

The Concept of Center

The word "center" is being used more and more frequently by performers to describe the point of origin of breathing, energy, and emotion. This concept is a pivotal one in martial arts philosophy and has gradually made its way into the study of theatre, dance, and sports throughout the world. Aikido practitioners call it the "one point," and locate it approximately an inch and a half below the navel. The followers of Ta'i Chi call it "Tan Tien," which means "Sea of Breathing." In Taoist terminology, center is likened to a stove where water boils and becomes steam.

In the early part of the twentieth century, the great director and teacher Constantin Stanislavsky told the Story of the Maharajah to introduce the concept of centering to acting students at the Moscow Art Theatre. It seems that the maharajah was looking for a new minister. He asked candidates to walk around the top of the city wall while carrying a dish of milk, full to the brim. The first candidate who could complete the walk without spilling the milk would be the new minister.

Distracted by the shouts of the crowd, the candidates all spilled the milk, and the maharajah sent them away. Then another candidate arrived and began his journey around the wall. As before, the people hooted and threw stones at him as he concentrated on his task. He was fired on by the troops, but to no avail. He completed his walk without spilling a drop. Asked later why the cries and shots hadn't disturbed him, the new minister replied, "I was watching the milk."

Neutral Position puts your body comfortably in alignment so that energy can flow through it freely. Finding your center enables you to get in touch with the source of that energy.

The concept of center is the foundation of poise and stage presence, the ability to hold an audience's attention and respect. "Centering" enables you to remain self-contained when other speakers seem to "lose it," "go to pieces," or "fall apart at the seams."

Centering For Performance

When actors discuss centering, they often use the term "in the moment." The term refers to that point in time when they "become" the characters, when nothing exists for them outside the play. The audience, the activities going on backstage, what they will do after the show—all disappear from their consciousness. Actors will tell you that when they are "in the moment," they do their best work.

Centering is like "Quality." It's almost impossible to define, but you know it when you see it. In class, after we have talked clients into Neutral Position, we introduce the concept of center. We bring it up casually, as though everyone already understands it. I'm always amazed to discover that everyone does already understand it. It appears that we are all intuitively aware of center, whether or not we've actually contemplated it before.

Whether or not you believe in center as a reality or locate it precisely isn't really important. If you go through the motions of centering yourself and act as though you're centered, you will be centered. Then nothing will matter except the activity you're engaged in at that moment. If you're speaking, your mind will be clear and calm, your body will operate at your command, and all the right words will come at the right time. Like the maharajah's minister, you will be unflappable. And your milk won't spill either.

Finding Center For Yourself

Once you've experienced the extraordinary sensation of being centered, I think you'll agree that it gives you immense personal power. You'll move in and out of Neutral Position often during a presentation, but you'll carry center with you all the time.

1. Stand in Neutral Position, with muscles relaxed. Pick a spot on the opposite wall at eye level and focus your attention on that spot.
2. Breathe easily and deeply (you don't need a lot of air, remember). Take a moment to quiet your thoughts. Then, gradually, begin to feel that place deep inside you that is your core, your "one point."
3. Count to ten, feeling your breath and the sound of your voice settling deep in your body.
4. As you count, allow yourself to sink into center. Quietly notice any tension creeping into your muscles and ease it away. Pay particular attention to your jaw, shoulders, hands, and knees.
5. When you are able to remain centered while you count, begin speaking. Introduce yourself to an imaginary group. This time look at them while you're speaking.
6. Move around the room, sit down in a chair or at your desk. Pick up a pen and write with it, staying centered while you move. If you feel yourself losing the sense of the exercise, stop, breathe, recenter, and start again.

Taking Command

When you are centered, you're able to take command of yourself and of your audience. A friend of mine, a theatre director who personally welcomes the audience before each play, confided his secret to me one evening after an especially fine introduction. "When I arrive onstage," he said, "I look out over the audience, center myself, and silently say to them: 'For these few moments, you are mine.'" He went on to describe how, by doing this, he put himself in complete charge. The audience responded by quieting, and he could then set the stage for the theatrical experience ahead. What my friend instinctively understands is the power of taking command and the difference between "command" and "control."

If I say to you, "Anne is a very controlled person," what is your image of Anne? Most likely you see Anne as rigid, stiff, unfeeling, perhaps even robotlike. That is because the concept of "control" is closed and defensive; it stops the flow of energy.

In contrast, if I tell you that Anne is always "in command," you will probably have an entirely different picture of Anne, an Anne who is strong and dynamic, who is fully in charge, and is comfortable with herself.

During past presentations, chances are your goal was to stay in "control"...keep "control" of the situation...not lose "control." If so, your ego thoughts were in charge, and you were held hostage by your inner judges. When you are centered, ego thoughts and inner judges don't even enter your consciousness. You feel loose, comfortable, and at ease in your speaker role.

At Voice-Pro, we begin our classes with some of the simple breathing exercises you have already learned in this book. At first, these activities seem pointless and undignified to some of the participants. Their inner judges are still calling the shots and they're reluctant to let down their guard. Yet because the instructor is clearly in command, no one has ever refused to complete the exercises. She sets the tone of the class, determines the activities and, not surprisingly, everyone follows.

One way to practice taking command is by "Casting the Net." Begin a day or two before your presentation. Go into an empty room and, in your imagination, set the stage. Decide where you are going to stand, and stand there. Take a moment to center yourself. Look out over your imaginary audience; then grab hold of an imaginary net with both hands, fling it out over the audience, and let it settle. Take your time, there's no need to rush. When your audience is secure within your net, begin to speak. Repeat this exercise a number of times, until you feel comfortable and natural doing it. Then, when the moment of your presentation actually arrives and you are standing before the group, mentally cast out your net and let it settle. Both you and your audience will feel the calming effects of this exercise and, when you begin, you will have their attention.

The Relaxed State

Each of the components of relaxation that we've talked about in these chapters is complete in itself. Focus, tension release, breathing, home base, and centering—all can be practiced independently of the other and can be called upon any time you need to calm your nerves. Combined, they become an integrated whole that is the foundation of successful speaking—the relaxed state.

III

The Magical Instrument: Your Voice

7

Finding Your Natural Voice

Human speech is like a cracked kettle on which
we tap crude rhythms for bears to dance, while we
long to make music that will melt the stars.
— Gustave Flaubert,
MADAME BOVARY

Your voice is your vocal signature. It is distinctively yours, unique in the same way your handwriting is unique. When you use it correctly, your voice is perfect for you.

From what they hear in your voice, your audience will make strong judgments about you. They decide whether you know what you're talking about, whether you care about what you're saying, and whether they should listen. Your voice not only determines if you will be heard, it gives color and meaning to your words, and conveys subtle messages about you as a person.

In a class of salespeople, one manager had a hard time accepting the fact that the voice makes a powerful statement. He simply didn't believe it. A colleague had just finished a presentation and was working on a vocal problem when the manager broke in. "I don't see why you're so concerned with her voice," he said. She's just inexperienced and nervous. In time, she'll be fine." Since she was neither inexperienced nor particularly nervous, I asked him how he got that impression. "Well, it's not her voice," he sputtered. "It just...it's just...it's just the way she *sounds.*"

There's a strong, pleasing voice inside each and every one of us. But very few people, unless they're singers, actors, or broadcasters, use it to their best advantage. As a performer yourself, you need to develop your voice in the same way they do.

Understanding Your Voice

We're all born with the same equipment for producing sound—two lungs, a diaphragm, a larynx containing the vocal folds (better known as vocal cords), and a mouth where the sound comes out. The size and configuration of this mechanism is genetically determined, so in effect, your ancestors have given you a natural voice and predetermined whether it is high, low, rich and deep, or clear and flute-like.

Environment, however, has determined how you use your natural voice and has influenced how you actually sound. This is where the trouble usually begins. At some point in your life you adopted the inflections, rhythms, and sounds of someone else. Little children learn to produce sound by imitation, which is why the speech patterns of Bostonians differ from those of Chicagoans, who don't sound at all like people from Atlanta. If your parents had a nasal twang, you probably have one, too. In any case, you *learned* speaking patterns that resulted in either a pleasant sounding voice or one that makes you cringe when you hear it on tape.

Your Vocal Instrument

Your body is your vocal instrument. Well-played, this instrument produces a pure, full-bodied sound that is your natural voice. All sound-making instruments contain three major components: a source of energy or power, which we can call the "generator"; something that turns the energy into sound, which is the "vibrator"; and something that will amplify the vibrations and enrich the sound, known as the "resonator."

In order to free your natural voice and develop it fully, you must take three steps. First, *generate* power from your diaphragm; second, open your throat so air passes freely over your vocal folds, which are the *vibrators;* and third, resonate the sound "in the mask." The quality and power of your voice will improve dramatically when these three components function together naturally and without strain.

The Diaphragm As Generator

Very early in my singing career, I had a real problem with being heard. My voice had a wonderful lyric quality, but it wasn't very big. Teacher after teacher told me I had to work on creating more volume. So I kept trying to sing louder. I pushed and pushed from my throat. But, instead of getting stronger, my voice wore out altogether. In desperation, I consulted a doctor who spoke the words that would change my life.

"Carolyn," he said, "Most voice problems are caused by poor breathing. If you want to sing well the rest of your life, you had better learn to breathe." Breathing to speak, like breathing to sing and breathing to relax, starts in the diaphragm—the speaking muscle. This muscle is the power source for all human sound. Breathing from the diaphragm reduces strain on the throat muscles. It supports and projects your voice rather than squeezing it out.

The diaphragm is a dome-shaped muscle that stretches horizontally above the stomach and just below the lungs. It is actually the floor of the thoracic, or chest cavity, and the ceiling of the abdominal cavity. In natural, deep breathing the diaphragm moves up and down like a piston or plunger, deepening the thoracic cavity as it flattens with each inhaled breath.

Power and Projection

Most speakers know they are supposed to "project" so they can be heard clearly and comfortably in the back of a room. The question is: How do you *do* that? Projection means more than just throwing your voice; it means filling the room with your vocal presence. That's why rather than loudness or volume, I prefer to think of projection as developing vocal power—power originating from the diaphragm.

The two best exercises I have ever found for vocal power and projection are The Plunger and The Windbag. Exercises like these allow great classical singers to sing without strain for hours at a time and to project, sans microphone, over raging symphony orchestras into the farthest corners of immense concert halls. If The Plunger and The Windbag work for the Pavarottis of the world, they will work for you.

The Plunger

1. Review The Hiss, The Ha's, and The Blah's from Chapter 4. (Head floated; shoulders, throat, and jaw relaxed; breath sent down through your body and out the hole in your back.)
2. Pretend your body contains a Plunger—the old plumber's friend. Starting at the crown of your head, the Plunger's wooden handle fits right in front of your spine, with the rubber bell located directly under your sternum.

3. Hiss to the end of your breath, pushing down periodically on the Plunger with little spurts of energy. If you place your hands on your waist, you will feel your body expand as the Plunger action depresses your diaphragm.
4. Repeat the Hiss, this time pushing the Plunger down and holding it there until your breath is gone. If the diaphragm tries to resume its resting position, give the Plunger an extra push. Resist against the natural tendency of the diaphragm to relax upon exhalation.
5. Practice The Plunger, using all initial breathing exercises: The Hiss, Ha, Blah, and Blah Plus Ten.

Diaphragm action powers your voice much like paddling powers a canoe. Left alone, the canoe will drift with the action of the water. When you use your paddle to push against the water, the canoe moves forward. Push the Plunger down and keep it down until your phrase is completed and you need to take a breath. Your voice will be propelled out over the audience, all the way to the back of the room.

The Windbag

Imagine that it's your job, every Sunday afternoon during football season, to sing the National Anthem at a National Football League stadium. Not only must you sing this difficult piece with no help from fans or marching band, you must sing it all the way through in one breath. Right now, please take the breath you will need to do just that.

When we ask clients to do this, their hands clench, their chests puff out, and their shoulders go up. But when inhaling for projection, your shoulders should be quiet and relaxed. Only your middle should expand as your diaphragm moves down, deeper and deeper.

1. Bend over from your waist. Round your shoulders, collapse your chest, and let your arms hang loose and easy, monkey style, below your shoulders.
2. Pretend that a long soda straw runs into your mouth, down through the tubes, and empties out into your lower back.
3. Slurping the air in through the straw like soup, let it fill your lower back. The greater the inhalation, the deeper you'll feel it—all the way down to your toes.

4. Loose jaw, loose shoulders, collapsed chest. If you feel
   pressure anywhere, stop, shake out, and start over.

With every Windbag breath, take in a little more air than the last
time. The Windbag improves your speaking power by increasing your
vital capacity (the volume of air you inhale with any one breath). As
an added bonus it will increase your endurance in running, walking,
cycling, skiing, swimming, and all other aerobic activities.

The Vocal Folds As Vibrator

Air, powered by the diaphragm, moves through the larynx and
over the vocal folds, setting up vibrations that put sound waves in
motion. You can best help your vocal folds do their job by leaving
them alone. Any conscious attempt on your part to control this
vibration or to "make sound" will only cause strain.

Use the Hiss, Ha's, and Blah's to relax any tension in the larynx.
As you unhinge your jaw and let your mouth drop open on Ha and
Blah, the back of your throat will open, freeing the vocal passage-
ways from constriction. Then give a little push on the Plunger, and
just enough air will pass across the vocal folds to start the vibration.

Resonating "In the Mask"

The sound produced by your vocal folds is thin and weak until it
is amplified and resonated in the bones and cavities of your face.
Singers know the importance of resonance. They call it being "in the
mask" because the voice resonates in that part of the face covered by
a theatrical mask. Inside the mask, sound waves bounce from wall to
wall, producing overtones that give your voice richness and body.

In the human instrument, the primary resonators are the teeth,
the hard palate, the nose and cheekbones, and the sinuses. When
your voice is resonating correctly, you feel a buzz in the area of the
mask. Close your mouth (relaxed jaw, remember), give a little push
to the Plunger, say "hmmmm," and you should feel it. If there's no
buzz, try this.

The Gravity Assist

1. From a standing or sitting position, bend over and position your face parallel to the floor.
2. Let your face go slack and feel the pull of gravity on
   your muscles. Feel your cheeks loosen, your nose get

longer, and your lips fall forward. Drool on the floor if
you must.

3. Count to ten, letting the words fall into the front of
your face (the mask). You should feel the buzz as gravity pulls everything down.

4. Now sit or stand erect and count again, retaining the
tonal buzz in the mask of your face.

Common Vocal Problems

Most vocal problems are caused by strain. If you suffer chronic or
severe difficulties, you should of course see a physician or speech
pathologist. However, most of the "garden variety" problems that
handicap business speakers can be corrected by doing the exercises in
this book.

Hoarseness. A hoarse voice usually begins with a slight huskiness
and, without treatment, develops into a rough, gravelly condition.
It's often accompanied by chronic throat-clearing. When not med-
ically based, huskiness and hoarseness are almost always the result of
strain and overuse. Use the Plunger and open your throat.

Breathiness. The breathy voice lacks sound. Some movie, television, and radio personalities deliberately cultivate a breathy voice
because they think it sounds sexy. Mostly, it just sounds breathy.
Avoid pushing air over the vocal folds. Instead, put breath under the
Plunger and use it for support.

Harshness and Stridency. Harshness is usually associated with the
male voice, while stridency (or shrillness) is considered a female
trait. Occurring most often in people who are considered energetic,
excitable, and aggressive, harshness and stridency have much in
common. They are characterized by a loud, pushy quality that talks
"at" an audience, rather than "with" them. If this is a problem for
you, open your throat, use the Plunger, and place your voice in the
mask.

Thinness. If you've ever been told, "You sound so much younger
than you look," or, "You sound like a child," your voice is too thin. A
thin voice is not well supported. The Plunger works wonders for thin
voices. It's like you grew up overnight.

Nasality. Nasality refers to the pinched, tight sound you get when
you talk through your nose. It is the same sound that gives singers of
country music their distinctive twang.

Push down on the Plunger and open your throat to release the pinch. The nasality will go away, leaving the resonance undisturbed.

The "Prize Fight Tenor." The athlete who concentrates on upper body building sometimes develops a vocal problem I call the "Prize Fight Tenor." We hear it often in athletes-turned-broadcasters who speak with high, tinny voices. This vocal problem occurs when body building results in excessive pressure and strain on the throat muscles. Exercises for resonance and an open throat will help. To avoid developing a "Prize Fight Tenor," athletes in weight training must do everything possible to eliminate pressure on the throat and vocal folds during workouts.

8

Vocal Clarity and Expression

think of the great voices you have heard why did you
like them think about this carefully they excited you
with their words don't you agree when they were
happy they filled you with joy when they were angry
you knew it sometimes in their excitement their
words spilled over each other and you felt excited too
wow you thought this is great other times they mes-
merized you with their solemn tones also their secret
whispers when you hear a great voice you feel it in
your soul wouldn't you like to have a great voice

No one would actually write a paragraph like that. In reality, it would be filled with punctuation marks, thoughtfully placed to signal where to start reading and where to stop. Commas are a symbol of one kind of pause, while periods are another. The exclamation point is much more emphatic! And don't you read a sentence that ends with a period very differently from the way you read one that ends with a question mark? Semicolons, colons, capital letters, and dashes—all give you clues to the interpretation of the paragraph.

If you look at magazine ads, you'll see how colors and varying sizes and styles of print are used to catch your eye and make you want to read about—and buy—the products displayed there. When words are in print, visual interest must be added so the meaning and the emotional tone of those words are unquestionably clear to the reader.

Speaking is no different. The starting and stopping must be there. There can be no doubt about where the punctuation is—caps, commas, periods, question marks must be in their proper places. It should be easy for your audience to distinguish a lively, upbeat message from one that's more serious. But your audience can't see the color and punctuation of your speech on the printed page; they must hear it in your voice.

Many business speakers, under the pressure of performance, become reciters of neutral words rather than conveyors of meaningful information. One client was told by his boss, "When you talk to me, I can't tell whether you're giving me good news or bad news." Words spoken without expression lack meaning because they have no color.

For example, say, "We've sold 10,000 units this month," as if this were your best month ever. Now say the same words again, expressing this time that it's been the worst month ever. The second time your voice was quite different from the first. It rose and fell in different places. Your tone changed. You put emphasis on different words to change the month's sales results from good to bad. There are many other ways you can say these simple words—surprised, questioning, defensive, to name just a few—and each time your vocal expression will change to accommodate the new meaning.

Articulation

Articulation provides clarity. Nothing frustrates an audience more than having to struggle just to make out a speaker's words. Articulation is the process of shaping the stream of air (that you generate in the diaphragm and vibrate through your vocal folds) into distinguishable speech sounds. These sounds are fashioned into words which, if they're correctly pronounced, are easily recognized by the receiver.

Improved articulation comes from making adjustments in one or both of the two sound groups: vowels and consonants.

When you speak a vowel sound (*a, e, i, o,* or *u,* with *y* sometimes functioning as a vowel), your jaw should be relaxed and your mouth open, so the air passes through unimpeded. Vowels are free and open sounds. The Ha's and Blah's of Chapter 4 will help you loosen your jaw so your vowels are free and unobstructed.

The rest of the 26 letters in the alphabet, including y most of the time, are consonants. Consonants are "stopped" sounds. The air flow is interrupted by a movement of lips, tongue, teeth or palate in order to cut off the sound. Say the sound of the letter b (not the letter itself but its sound) a number of times: /b/ /b/ /b/ /b/. Now try /t/ /t/ /t/ /t/. You can both feel and hear the stopping of the sound.

Vowels spin out sound and consonants cut it off. If your speech is not as clear as you would like, look at words carefully and pronounce them so that each vowel is open and clear, and each consonant stops exactly as it is supposed to stop.

Read into a tape recorder and, if your b's aren't clear, practice saying words with lots of b's in them. If you have the flat aah sound of the upper Midwest (as in cat), unhinge your jaw and let the vowel open up. On your own, you can quite easily create exercises to correct your articulation problems.

Rate

By nature, some people think and act quickly, while others are slower and more deliberate. If you're a fast thinker, your rate of speech will be faster than average and will likely accelerate when you're under pressure; the more methodical person will slow down, often stopping between words to have more thinking time.

If you want to measure the rate of your speech, select a passage you're comfortable with and read it aloud for a period of two minutes. Count the number of words you read and divide by two to get your rate per minute. The average rate of conversational speech is 120 to 125 words per minute. Reading out loud goes slightly faster, between 150 and 180 words per minute. After you test yourself two or three times to make sure you're being accurate, you'll know if you need to adjust your rate up or down.

Speakers who talk too fast are usually trying to keep pace with their thoughts, which flow at a considerably faster rate than the spoken word. Words need to stay in the moment, in the "here and now" so your audience has time to comprehend your message. If you talk as fast as you think, you'll leave them in the dust. Simply making a decision to "talk slower this time" doesn't work. You need to give yourself something to do so it actually takes longer to get the words out.

First, make sure you're articulating clearly. E-nun-ci-ate e-ver-y syl-la-ble of e-ver-y word. Complete each word before you go on to the next word. Speakers in a hurry often say only about half of each word and are amazed to hear how sloppy they sound when they're recorded on tape.

The next step in slowing down is to phrase correctly. In a written text, your eye absorbs punctuation marks, even though you're not conscious of them. Since the spoken word must be punctuated too, pause slightly for commas, longer for periods, and stop for a full beat at the end of a paragraph. These little pauses use up time and result in a much more moderate rate of speech.

If you are a slower, more deliberate speaker, do the opposite. Avoid *overphrasing* by learning to speak in complete ideas rather than single words. Read aloud, keeping your energy moving all the way to the end of a phrase or sentence, and don't stop until you reach the punctuation mark. Feel the sweep of the line and match your words to it.

Instead of:
When/the report/is finished/I will/take it/to the printer.
say:
When the report is finished/I will take it to the printer.

Another way to speed up your speech is to learn to "beat the clock." Set a timer for a period of one minute. Read aloud at a rate that feels comfortable to you and, when the timer goes off, mark your ending place. Now mark a spot ten words farther on and reread the passage, aiming for the new mark at the end of a minute. Keep moving the mark until you can easily read 200 words in your one-minute time span. Since conversational speech is slower than that, it will be easy for you to relax back into a rate that is comfortable for both you and your audience.

Pitch, Range, and Inflection

Pitch refers to whether a particular sound is high or low. Your voice has a natural pitch level and a basic range of pitch that is determined by the structure of your larynx. The longer the vocal folds, the lower the pitch, which is why men generally have lower voices than women.

You can find your natural pitch level in the same way you tested for resonance in the mask. Keep your jaw relaxed, close your mouth lightly, give a gentle Plunge, and say, "hmmmm." Now count to ten on that pitch. Does your voice resonate easily and without strain? If so, that is your natural pitch level. When you are speaking correctly, your tone will hover somewhere around that pitch.

Inflection is variation of pitch, or stringing together a group of pitches to form a melodic line. Unfortunately, many speakers use relatively little inflection, sometimes none at all. Speech without inflection is not only more difficult to understand, it's boring to listen to. At one time or another we've all been lulled to sleep by a speaker with a monotone voice. The full use of your vocal range, with all its high's and low's, adds color that captures and holds your listeners' attention. Most people have a much wider vocal range than they realize and are capable of using a lot more inflection than they do.

The following exercises are good for increasing vocal flexibility and extending your range. You can also read aloud, especially to children, putting more and more inflection into your voice with each story.

The Siren

1. Find your natural pitch level. Relax your jaw, close your mouth lightly, give a gentle Plunge, and say, "hmmmm."
2. Sustain the tone and move the pitch up and down your range—like a miniature siren. Go as high and as low as you comfortably can, gradually extending both upper and lower limits of your range.
3. As your voice goes up in pitch, push a bit more on the Plunger to give it the support it needs. Keep your jaw relaxed and avoid any tension in your throat.

The 10-Count Siren

1. Count to ten, placing each number on a different pitch. Make sure you place at least one number at the high end of your range and one number at the low end.
2. Repeat several times, smoothing out the tone until the *10-count* takes on the character of a real sentence.

Number-Talk

1. Imagine you are speaking to an audience in a foreign country where the language is Number-Talk. Practice your speech, using numbers instead of words.
2. Let your voice go where it needs to go in order to get your point across. Make yourself understood.

Phrase Terminals

Ask the question, "Would you like to go swimming?" and you will hear the pitch of your voice lift at the end of the sentence. Now say, "I want that report, and I want it now." This time your voice most emphatically went down.

A phrase terminal is a rising or falling pitch at the end of a phrase or sentence that gives the listener extra information about the speaker's meaning. If your pitch goes up, you sound tentative, questioning, uncertain, as if you are asking permission all the time. Your introduction may go something like this: Good morning? I'm John Smith? Vice President of the XYZ Corporation? Chemical waste must be disposed of properly? At XYZ we do it right? You can count on us?

Dropping the pitch at the end of a phrase conveys certainty and authority. When you let your voice drop, you'll come across as strong and confident. Surprisingly, the pitch drop is also an effective way to end a question. Drop the pitch when you ask, "When will that report be ready?" and everyone will know you mean business.

Emphasis and Topping

By putting extra stress on certain syllables, you are able to give prominence to important words. By "leaning" on words, you can even change the meaning of an entire sentence.

> *I* didn't say you took the money.
> I *didn't* say you took the money.
> I didn't *say* you took the money.
> I didn't say *you* took the money.
> I didn't say you *took* the money.
> I didn't say you took the *money.*

Topping is a specific acting technique for building to a vocal climax. Use it to make a list, a series, or a sequence more compelling. The trick is to speak each element of the series in a slightly different way. You can crescendo (get louder) to the end, or you can decrescendo (get softer). You can speed up as you move through the list, or slow down and pause when you get to the last...word. Whatever you do, the idea is to move the series to its conclusion, emphasizing each word in a way that it upstages, or "tops," the previous word.

In Shakespeare's *King Lear*, Lear mourns over the body of his daughter Cordelia, saying, "Thou'lt come no more, never, never, never, never, never." There are as many ways of speaking that line as there are actors to play Lear, but each word must build up...or build down...to a riveting climax.

The Pause That Speaks

Too many speakers are afraid of silence. The thought of appearing to lose their place or not knowing what to say next fills them with dread. These speakers fill empty spaces with "ah's" and "uh's," coughs, nervous giggles, and other distracting fillers. They ramble on, bombarding their listeners with sounds, when often they should just…stop…talking.

Pauses stimulate attention by allowing the audience time to digest what you've said and anticipate what's to come. They give you recovery time, a quiet moment to relax, breathe, and gather your thoughts. During pauses, you and your audience actually have time to look at each other, which gives you a good opportunity to make connection. It helps to think of pauses not as breaks in momentum, but as an integral part of the music of speech. They are bridges, not empty spaces. Your energy level doesn't die; it moves forward to the conclusion of an idea. I learned as a musician: "Sing through your rests." Let the silence ring with eloquence. Daring to pause adds drama to your speaking because it is so rare.

Foreign and Regional Accents

I recently conducted a seminar for a corporate client whose chairman, born and raised in Germany, spoke with a heavy accent. He was concerned that people had difficulty understanding him, and he wanted to "fix his accent." When I worked with Carl, I found that his speaking problem had nothing at all to do with his accent. Because he spoke much too fast and ran his words together, Carl was unintelligible in any language. He was able to eliminate the "accent problem" by developing a more moderate rate and articulating each and every word.

I like regional and foreign accents because, in our ever more homogenized society, they breathe of freshness and individuality. If you worry that people aren't able to understand you because of an accent, don't make the mistake of trying to rid yourself of it completely. Instead, breathe, pace yourself, unhinge your jaw, and articulate. In most cases, when you fix the technique, you fix the accent.

Once More With Feeling

If these, and other, exercises seem mechanical, it's because they are. Musicians spend a significant amount of time in the mechanical practice of scales, not because they want to play scales beautifully, but because the practice helps them perfect their technique. Developing vocal technique also takes practice, and it's the repetition and drill that ultimately establishes new, more interesting speaking patterns.

But as you know, the subject of your presentation isn't your technical prowess. So as soon as you have mastered a vocal technique, throw it away. Don't try to incorporate it *mechanically* into your speeches. At performance time, look at the people in the audience and, quite simply, talk to them. The punctuation, precision, rhythm, and color you have practiced will all be there, naturally and without effort from you.

IV

Body Magic

9

Freeing Your Body For Movement

A number of years ago, as part of my work with a regional theatre company, I went into English classes to introduce high school seniors to the excitement of live Shakespeare. At one school, my partner and I had already completed three performances. Hot, tired, and by that time just going through the motions, we were perfunctorily readying ourselves for a fourth when the teacher remarked, "Oh, by the way, three quarters of the students in this class are deaf."

Deaf??? "Where's the guy who does the sign language?" my partner cried. But there was no guy who did the sign language. It was up to the two of us to make Julius Caesar understood and enjoyed by 24 young people, 18 of whom couldn't hear us.

It turned out to be a wonderful performance. Forced to communicate through physical means alone, we were more expressive in that class than we had been all day. Each movement was clear and connected to Shakespeare's words. The play came alive and the kids loved it.

I learned an important lesson that day. Dynamic performers communicate with their entire bodies. They use movement to underline, punctuate, and bring meaning to their words. The best speakers come alive through physical expression that is both spontaneous and purposeful. And because their vitality is natural and consistent with their personalities, their work appears effortless.

No one can teach you exactly how to use your body when you speak. There are no right and wrong ways to move. There are, however, movements that feel comfortable and enhance your message, and movements that look awkward and are distracting to your audience. This chapter will help you free your body for movement so you can discover for yourself the postures and gestures that feel right, look good, and work for you.

As I've said before, business speakers often suffer from a need to overcontrol. The result is a stiff performance, with the speaker expressionless and frozen in place. Over and over I hear comments like: "I'm afraid I'll look phony." "I've watched other speakers try to be animated, and they just look silly." "I'll feel like a dope if I do that." The fear of looking silly in front of your peers is a valid concern. But there is a way to reconcile it with the very real need for you to express yourself physically when you speak.

The secret to dynamic performance is to do everything you possibly can to free up your body *before you speak*. Experiment with physical expression and let go of your inhibitions—*in practice*. Then, when you find yourself in a real performance, you'll be comfortable with movement. Instinctively you'll incorporate the actions that accurately express your message.

Freeing Your Body for Movement

Begin by doing *The Shake*. In Chapter 4 the purpose of The Shake was to help you relax by loosening your muscles. In this chapter it has a somewhat different function—to get your body moving and to directly address your fear of looking and feeling silly when you move. Now is the time to deal with your inner judges, once and for all. Round them up and put them in a drawer someplace, while you take time out for play.

1. Wiggle your fingers. Then add your hands, and shake them too.
2. Add, one by one, your elbows, chest, waist, hips, knees, and feet, until you're shaking all over.
3. Let your head move with your body, then add your voice, shaking body and voice all the way down to your toes. Let yourself go. Feel what it's like to move without inhibition. Remember, you're not expected to do The Shake before a live audience. This is only for practice.

One of the most expressive artistic forms is pantomime. The best way I know to learn to express ideas physically is to take away the words, which is what happened when Bernie and I performed Shakespeare for deaf teenagers. When a good mime performs, we see every detail of the story without any need for words. You can experiment with mime on your own. Demonstrate that you're happy.

What happened to your body? To your face? Now show that you're sad. What physical changes did you feel? Act out *scared, curious, angry, tired.* Like the mime, you don't need words to be understood. As you experiment, try to avoid stock gestures of cliche. Let your movement flow out of your inner feelings about words like scared or curious.

Mime has been popularized in the party game "Charades." Some people love to play Charades and are pretty good at it. Others hate it. If you hate Charades, you probably need to play it more. But whether or not you're good at Charades doesn't really matter. The real question is, can you put aside any concern you may have for your professional dignity and act goofy in a group of other goofy people? If you can, it will become easier and easier for you to be naturally expressive in other, more professional situations.

Become a Storyteller

A very good way to free yourself up for physical expression is to tell stories and act them out. But don't just talk, show what's going on. Pretend you are entertaining small children. (If you have small children handy, you can have great fun practicing with them.)

An attorney found acting out stories especially difficult. Dave felt his law firm would frown on such antics. Finally, he let himself go and, to everyone's enjoyment, acted out an unusually corny story. Later, he was able to incorporate the same sort of natural expression into a real presentation. At rehearsal, members of his firm broke into applause. Asked later what caused the breakthrough, he said, "I decided to perform for my colleagues the same way I perform for my kids." Dave had all the tools to be a dynamic speaker but, prior to this, the controls he put on himself had inhibited him in his performances.

To Move Or Not To Move

At a recent conference, I watched and listened to the keynote speaker, a magnificent performer. During her presentation she was all over the stage. She stood behind the podium, she moved out to stand closer to the audience, she leaned against a table, and she often walked across the platform to refer to her charts. Once she even sat on the edge of the stage. Each movement was full of purpose and her gestures were expansive. Her face was alive, her eyes sparkled, and she captivated the audience with her vitality and charm.

At lunch I quizzed those at my table as to why they felt this speaker had been so effective. "Was it the way she moved?" "Oh no," the answer came. "She really didn't move much. She was just fun to listen to." This woman had been in motion almost constantly, yet the audience really didn't notice it.

Any movement is appropriate if it's connected to your meaning and doesn't distract the audience. If you stand on your head and the audience says, "Wow, now I understand!", your choice was good because, from their point of view, the action fit the message. If you stand on your head and they wonder what you're doing that for, your choice was wrong for that particular message and that particular audience.

When you want to direct your remarks to one part of the audience, walk over to them. When you want to refer to a chart, go there. If you are behind a table or lectern and wish to be closer to your listeners, position yourself *decisively* where you want to be. The speaker who paces back and forth, or drifts aimlessly about, can drive an audience crazy. If there's no reason for you to move, **stand still.**

Clients are often skeptical when I tell them that aimless drifting or rhythmic pacing detracts from their message. "Walking is interesting," they tell me. Yes, walking is interesting, but only if it is connected to the meaning of your words and clearly defines and punctuates your ideas. You must actually go somewhere. The caged-tiger-pacing back-and-forth of many business presenters is most often just a release of nervous energy. Better to breathe, center yourself, and move for a purpose, than to drive people to distraction or put them to sleep with hypnotic movement.

Movement can be used to signal a change of ideas. "We've talked about this. Now let's talk about that." With a shift of position on the second sentence, you let the audience know it's time to shift gears. Beware, however, the debater's technique of "three steps and plant" that occurs with *every* change of ideas. If it becomes repetitious, an action loses its effectiveness.

Filling Your Space

One client, a securities analyst, was a real "shrinking violet." Already petite, Susan seemed to shrink into herself when she spoke before an audience, as if she was trying to take up less space or even make herself disappear.

She kept her chin down and her shoulders scrunched. Her elbows were glued to her sides, which kept her gestures small and close to her body. We told Susan to fill the space around her—to reach out into the space and own it. Almost immediately her physical presence grew. She took on an air of greater power and authority, and her gestures became more expansive. She could feel the difference and so could her audience.

Filling your space is a mental concept that lets you be comfortable speaking in rooms of any size and allows you to move with greater ease and freedom. You can practice by standing or sitting in a chair, then drawing an imaginary circle closely around you. Mentally fill the space within the circle. Now, in your imagination, enlarge the space by moving out the circle. Then fill that space. Expand your presence within continually widening circles until your personal space encompasses the entire room.

Get Out of Your Comfort Zone

Your experimentation with movement and physical expression should take you out of your "comfort zone." If you have a tendency toward overcontrol, your expressive comfort zone is very small, and it may be uncomfortable, even scary, for you to expand your boundaries into new territory. But it's worth it, and the results may surprise you.

Clients, who are convinced that their wild shenanigans are way out of line, are amazed to find they look perfectly normal when they see themselves on videotape. What feels like excessive exaggeration to them is really within the realm of acceptable business speaking. Once you realize you're still working within acceptable limits, you can practice expressive behavior until it begins to feel natural, enlarging your comfort zone as the new habits take over.

When you first move into this unfamiliar territory, it's essential to get feedback from people you trust. The reaction of Dave's colleagues to his new style reassured him that he hadn't gone too far. Videotape doesn't lie and can be a terrific learning tool. A friend can give you a secret signal if you seem to be hamming it up. The advice of a good coach outside your organization can be especially valuable.

But overdoing it is rarely a problem and, if you do end up giving too much, it's always easy to pull back. You have an innate sense of good taste. If you're comfortable with physical expression and feel free to move when and how your speech dictates, your own sense of truth will be your best guide.

10

Body Talk

No mortal can keep a secret. If his lips are silent, he chatters with his finger tips; betrayal oozes out of every pore!
—Sigmund Freud

All of us are more sensitive than we realize to the nonverbal signals of others. Nonverbal communication, or what we have come to call body language, is extremely powerful because it is interpreted primarily in the subconscious mind, while words communicate mainly with the conscious mind. In most cases your audience gives more weight to your actions than to your words, which means that, if your actions contradict your words, your spoken message will be doubted, or even disregarded altogether.

While it's a mistake to isolate a single gesture and declare, unequivocally, that it has a specific meaning, there is evidence that people respond positively to certain *patterns* of behavior, and negatively to others. Open, erect, relaxed posture and movement, for example, are usually considered strong and confident. Slumped, defensive postures, particularly where there is no eye contact, will appear weak and evasive. And a speaker's behavior that seems to invade anyone's personal space, including a pointing finger, a jutting jaw, and standing or walking too close to the audience, is usually construed as threatening.

As you become more aware of your own physical mannerisms, you may discover that they are sometimes in conflict with both your intended message and the overall impression you want to make. When this conflict occurs, you'll end up confusing your audience, and they may respond in surprising ways. Michael, a financial manager, came to me after overhearing a disturbing comment during one of his presentations. He had been speaking during a strategy session that would eventually lead to massive layoffs, when he heard someone remark, "I can't figure out what this guy thinks is so funny." No one seemed to recognize Michael's genuine concern for the state of his company, and he didn't know why. As we worked together I could see that physical tension was causing his face to lock in a grin. The result was that in serious situations, Michael sent perplexing mixed messages to his audience.

Audience understanding comes when you deliver a unified message. That only happens when your voice, your facial expression, your gestures, and your actions clearly reinforce the message you wish them to hear.

Years of listening to feedback about my own presentations has taught me that people tend to see me as a powerful, sometimes rather imposing figure. In a formal setting, or if I'm addressing a group of tough-minded executives, that's fine. At other times, when I want to establish a warmer, more casual relationship with my audience, I've found that my direct, no-nonsense attitude can backfire, and I need to change the *way* I deliver my words. So I've learned to soften my image by shifting my position off center, sliding a hand in my pocket, and making sure that, in my intensity, I don't forget to smile.

Put On a Real Face

Audiences notice your face first. The expression on your face influences them more than anything else about you, including the content of your presentation. Your facial expression must grow out of the emotional commitment you feel for your subject and your audience. Your face will be alive and expressive, and your smile sincere, if you allow yourself to feel the emotion of your message and respond to it "in the moment." Yet many speakers, under the pressure of performance, forget that audiences respond to the face first. They forget to smile.

The smile on a *real* face is a genuine smile. You can try to fake it by artificially arranging your facial muscles, but you'll only end up with a dreadful "plastic" grin. You can try to look pleasant while your fists and teeth remain clenched, but you'll find it's an impossible task. If, instead of manipulating your facial muscles into an empty grimace, you change your mindset and think of the audience as an honored guest, your pleasure in speaking to them will show naturally in your face. When they laugh at something you've said, a twinkle in your eye will tell them you honestly share their enjoyment. A genuine smile happens when you're able to relax and let your inner energy light your face and your personal warmth glow in your eyes.

Of course, as Michael learned, it's not always appropriate to smile. A serious subject should be accompanied by a facial expression that accurately represents the gravity of the situation. There are also times, especially during negotiation, when it's advantageous to show a neutral face to your audience. This is perfectly okay, as long as the choice you've made is a strategic one.

Beware, however, of the "Great Stone Face," a face that is *unintentionally* without expression or emotion. A direct result of overcontrol, the "Great Stone Face" goes hand in hand with the monotone voice and closed posture of so many business speakers. "The Great Stone Face" is dangerous because, no matter how many magnificent words pour from a speaker's lips, in the minds of the audience a blank face communicates a blank mind.

Modifying Your Image

An open posture is powerful. It seems to say, "Go ahead and shoot your arrows at me. I can take it." Neutral Position, as I described in Chapter 5, is the classic open posture. With your shoulders down, chest open, and head floating, you'll send a message that you're both powerful and approachable. Standing in Neutral Position with your feet shoulder-width apart and your weight evenly distributed also grounds you, but at the same time leaves you prepared to move freely in any direction.

Closed posture, on the other hand, causes you to lose power. Clasping your hands behind your back is more closed than you might think, because it inhibits movement and blocks opportunities for expression. Folding your arms across your body is also a closed, "I don't want to be here" posture. Standing with your feet together narrows and weakens you, making you look as though you could easily be toppled over. And when you clasp your hands in front of your crotch in what is known as the "fig leaf," you'll look awkward and uncomfortable, even giving the audience the impression that you're sheepish and embarrassed.

If you want to move out of neutral position in order to soften your message, there are a number of ways to do it so that you stay open to the audience. Shifting your weight onto one foot, for example, is a relaxed and natural way to create a casual atmosphere. You might also think about putting a hand in your pocket. This, of course, assumes that your hand is relaxed. If you're hiding twitchy fingers or nervously playing with keys or change, you won't be able to establish the relaxed atmosphere you're after. Instead of hiding your nervousness, you'll just call attention to it. Some experts will tell you that putting a hand in your pocket is something only men should do. I don't agree. It works for me—and for a female state legislator in our area who fields tough questions in a relaxed, casual stance with at least one hand in her pocket. She always appears comfortable, no matter how tense the situation.

"What Do I Do With My Hands?"

All speech consultants hear that question over and over. Although the best answer is, "Forget about them and let them do what comes naturally," that's not much help if you're self-conscious about your hands and don't know whether to use them or hide them away. Like your face, your hands are wondrous tools for expression. Use them to emphasize your words and paint visual pictures in the minds of your listeners.

If you're one of those people who gesture a lot but have been told since childhood not to talk with your hands, don't despair. You can use your hands as much as you like, as long as your gestures mean something and are connected to your message. During practice, put meaning into your gestures by drawing objects in the air as you talk about them. Describe your desk, using your hands to create the smooth top surface. Show us the four legs. Open and close an imaginary drawer. Actors in training spend hours doing this, and you can take advantage of the same technique to make your own gestures more definitive and precise.

In general, open hands carry a positive connotation. Historically, men of good will have extended their right hands in greeting, with palms open to display the absence of a weapon. The open hand is still a traditional signal of sincerity and lack of concealment. A sweeping, palm-up gesture on the words "all of you" is more inviting than a palm-down, pointing finger.

Of course, your intended message may not necessarily be open and inviting. "We will not be deterred from our goal," is better said with palms down, physical emphasis added on the word "not." Pointing to a chart is also much stronger if you point with your palm down and the back of your hand turned up toward the audience.

You can use your hands to indicate size. I often demonstrate by using this example: "There is a meadow, with waving grasses and brilliantly colored flowers, and in the corner of the meadow is a pond." By moving both hands to one side and creating a small circle with them, I give the impression of a small pond. The second time I describe the meadow, I keep one hand in front of me and move the other far to the side. With my hands in the same circle-like position, I have now created a very large pond. The audience clearly sees the two ponds and has no trouble differentiating between the two in their minds. I haven't given verbal dimensions of the pond—in this case it doesn't matter—but I've made its relative size very clear.

You can also use your hands to indicate distance and direction. Exactly how high is "high"? Let your audience know, not by telling them in endless detail, but by showing them. In class, I occasionally experiment with directional gesturing. Holding my elbow close to my side, I flap my hand weakly and say, "Now let them hear your words in the parking lot." Seldom do we hear much change in the client's projection. Then I say it again, this time with my arm out straight, finger pointed, with physical emphasis on the words "parking lot." The change that takes place always amazes us. The client responds to my more emphatic gesture in dramatic fashion, with a voice that suddenly projects power and energy.

Sometimes people get in the habit of rhythmically beating time to their words, both hands going at the same time. Beware of any repetitious gesture. Like caged-tiger pacing, any action done over and over calls attention to itself and eventually lulls the audience into inattention.

Don't Plan Your Gestures

If your body is relaxed and you've experimented with freedom of movement, as I suggested in Chapter 9, your gestures will occur spontaneously. You won't have to think them up in advance. When you look out at the audience, imagine they are commanding you:

"Show me." Then use all of you—your face, your body, your hands—to paint clear visual pictures for them. This chapter describes only some of the choices you can make when it comes to body talk. Just remember that "natural" is the key.

I never prescribe gestures for clients and I strongly advise against your planning them ahead of time because *planned gestures look phony.* Audiences are astute. They recognize when gestures have been rehearsed and they feel manipulated. Besides, a live presentation to a live audience is much different from a practice session, and a gesture that works in rehearsal may not work at all when you're in front of an audience.

Tempting as it may be, don't practice at all in front of a mirror. Using a mirror in rehearsal distorts your mental focus because it requires you to play the role of both speaker and audience. It takes away from the naturalness and spontaneity you're striving for and, as a recurring practice tool, will have a negative impact on your presentation.

11

Your Physical Presence

Your physical presence is more than just your outward appearance, though that's a big part of it. You are the sum total of your health, your fitness level, and your personal style. Each contributes to the image you carry with you to the speaker's platform, and each is important in its own way.

A throughline of this book is that your preparation for speaking should include the same devotion to training that athletes and other performers give to their work. A good stage or screen performance requires a high level of physical fitness, and dedicated actors watch their diets, work out religiously, and make sure they remain in top physical condition.

Why shouldn't the same be true for you? When you give an hour-long presentation, or conduct a seminar, or facilitate an all-day meeting, it's as if you were giving a one-man show. If you expect to hold out, and hold an audience for that length of time, you need energy and stamina. So your training should take into account diet and exercise, along with careful attention to your appearance.

Eating to Speak

I don't think I'm being terribly controversial when I say that much of what we eat is bad for us. And what's bad for us as human beings is especially bad for us as performers. Fats and sugars create bulges in the wrong places and give skin an unhealthy, pasty look. They also provide no lasting energy, as anyone who has suffered a sugar crash in the middle of a lengthy marketing report can attest. Coffee and donuts aren't likely to carry a person through a morning of normal workloads, let alone provide the fuel a speaker needs when the adrenalin starts to pump.

I'm a firm believer in the benefits of good nutrition. And I'm convinced that the diets of athletic achievers on tennis courts and ski slopes are perfect for my clients who spend so much of their time in high-stakes communication with others. You may not need as *much* food as an Olympic skier, but you need the same kind of food. Lots of whole grains, fruits, and vegetables, moderate amounts of protein and dairy products, light on the fat, and as little refined sugar as you can let yourself get by with.

I get a lot of questions about what to eat right before a speaking performance. My own preference is for something bland—a piece of broiled chicken, a baked potato with some yogurt topping, and a vegetable of some kind. It's pretty boring, but it's guaranteed not to set my stomach gurgling. I try to avoid big salads right before I speak, and I always save the Szechwan and Mexican dishes for another, more favorable time.

Another question that often comes up has to do with whether or not it's okay to drink milk before you speak. Some of my clients find they have to continually clear their throats after they've consumed milk or other dairy products. Concert singers rigorously protect themselves against this dreaded "throat phlegm" by avoiding milk for hours before they sing. If you struggle with chronic throat congestion, check to see if milk might be the cause. If it is, avoiding dairy products becomes an easy solution to an exasperating problem.

A word about caffeine. Some people tolerate it well and some don't. As with any dietary change, you must always experiment until you find what works for you. But if you suffer from extreme performance anxiety and the butterflies seem to get the best of you despite all the deep breathing you do, you'd best cut down on coffee, tea, and colas.

New clients who come to me for help with stagefright sometimes confess that they're tempted to take a drink now and then before a speech. It's easy at a convention or dinner meeting to accept a highball or a glass of wine, telling yourself it will relax you and help you do a better job. Well, while it may relax you, it's more likely to put you to sleep than help you do a better job of speaking. You want your mind sharp when you're the presenter, and alcohol never satisfies the need to think clearly. The same is true for any drug that claims to anesthetize you to the pain of stagefright. Learn to relax yourself through the natural methods you've learned in earlier chapters, and leave the drugs alone.

Ice is Not Nice

Gerald came into class thinking he had a problem with nerves. A frequent conference speaker, he looked forward to his presentations and suffered no pre-performance jitters at all. But he gradually noticed that a few minutes into a speech, his throat would begin to tighten, and by the time he was finished he could hardly get the words out. "How can I feel this nervous," he moaned, "when I'm not really nervous at all?"

This one was easy. All conference centers, hotels, and dining rooms graciously provide pitchers full of ice water on the tables and at the podium. Gerald, sipping innocently away, was unknowingly creating his own problem.

As matter cools, it contracts and gets smaller. The atoms and molecules that vibrated vigorously when the matter was warm begin to slow down and move closer together. This is why, when you put ice on a bruise, you will reduce the swelling. And that's exactly what happens in your throat when ice and cold water move across your delicate vocal folds. They tighten and, like a tense, cold muscle, refuse to do the work for which they're needed.

The solution to Gerald's problem was simply to exchange the pitcher of ice water for one in which the water was room temperature, or even a little bit warm. The result? No constricted throat, no pushed words, and a much happier conference speaker.

Keeping Fit to Speak

Because so much of our class work begins with breathing, I'm a fervent advocate of aerobic training. Walking, running, cycling, swimming, cross country skiing—I do them all, and I'm convinced that being aerobically fit allows me to speak and teach with much more vigor than I might otherwise have.

The term "aerobic" means "utilizing oxygen." Aerobic exercises are endurance exercises that increase the body's ability to move air into and out of the lungs. At the same time the total blood volume in the body increases, which increases the amount of oxygen that is transported through the system. The results of aerobic exercise are: more energy, stronger bones, greater ability to handle stress, and better concentration at work.

I can tell in the first five minutes of my work with clients if they're in good condition. When they're already committed to long-term aerobic training, my job is so much easier. There's no need for weeks of breathing exercises, and we can move on quickly to the more expressive aspects of presentation.

Aerobic training will also strengthen your legs, another critical area of a performer's body. If you're a teacher, trainer, a trial lawyer, or anyone else whose speaking time is spent on your feet, it's critical that you take care of that precious base of yours. An old German tenor was once asked how long he would be able to sing. "The voice goes on forever," he replied, "aber die beine, die beine!" ("But the knees, the knees!")

Your Appearance

There isn't space here for a thorough discussion of how to choose a business wardrobe. Besides, there are some excellent books already available on this subject. There are also, in some industries and some regions of the country, unspoken conventions that may limit the choices you have. So it's a good idea, when you're starting out with a company, to pay close attention to the style in which people dress and the message that style conveys about both the company itself and the people who work there. That knowledge should form the basis for the selection of your business wardrobe.

When it's time to decide what to wear for a presentation, think about two things. First, don't stray too far from your own personal style. If you normally dress in a conservative, classic fashion, don't change it in an attempt to somehow be more dramatic, or because the high school kids you're speaking to will all be in jeans and tee shirts.

Second, within the bounds of appropriateness, dress to fit the occasion and the audience. For men this often isn't difficult because a conservative business suit is a conservative business suit and is appropriate at a morning meeting, at lunch with the CEO, or at a prestigious professional dinner. However, that dark blue suit, white shirt, and maroon tie won't look nearly as good when your presentation is scheduled for 11:00 Saturday morning, to be followed by the annual golf outing. Then a pair of slacks, a polo shirt, and a sport coat will look much better.

Women have a much wider variety of choices when it comes to what to wear, which means there are more decisions to be made and more chances for error. But here again, a thorough knowledge of the basic principles of business dress, plus a clear understanding of the customs within your own workplace will lighten the burden. If you're speaking in a conservative setting, you'll never go wrong in a classic suit and silk blouse. For a while, that was practically all a woman could wear if she wanted to be seen as credible. But the rules have relaxed over the years, and now a well-cut business dress is equally acceptable.

In order to keep things simple and not get hung up on lists of rules about dress that can pull your focus away from your audience and end up paralyzing you with indecision, I have three suggestions you can apply anywhere in any situation: Dress up a little more than your audience, make sure your clothes are comfortable and fit well, and always wear expensive underwear.

Dress Up More Than Your Audience

Dressing up a little more than your audience will set you apart from the group and add to your credibility. This is especially true for a woman. If *they're* in jeans, then *you* wear slacks and a stylish blouse or top. If they're dressy casual in slacks, put on a skirt or dress. If they're in conservative business suits, add flair to yours by selecting one that's brightly colored, or wearing a blouse or scarf in a bold print.

You can also dress up for your audience by wearing the same type of clothing but in a dressier fabric. I once observed a speaker addressing a group of women business owners. She wore a classic business suit, but when I spoke to her afterwards, I realized that it was made of a rich blue velvet. She sent us all the elegant message, "I'm with you but I'm special."

Eyeglasses are a part of your wardrobe. If you normally wear glasses or contact lenses, you'll want to wear them while you speak— with two exceptions. Avoid tinted lenses, which may darken and cause your audience to lose contact with you. And don't perform in half-glasses, which will make you look patronizing and haughty.

Wear Clothes That Fit

The way your clothes fit is far more important than their style or how much you paid for them. Most of my clients know what to wear, but many of them aren't aware of how they really look. It's so easy to keep wearing an outfit, even though you've added enough pounds to throw you into the next size up. Does your jacket button without pulling? Will your arms move freely when you gesture? Do your hemlines hang straight or do your skirts or slacks get hung up around unsightly bulges? Invest in a good mirror and find out.

I once took two pairs of new shoes on a speaking tour. I won't do that again. The fit of your shoes is an important consideration, especially for women. Make sure your shoes are well broken in so they don't pinch. Mid-size heels are universally accepted for women's business footwear. They're much more attractive than flats and easier to walk in than higher heels.

Always Wear Expensive Underwear

A canny, old salesman shared his secret of success with me one evening after an all-day meeting. "I get to know my customers," he confided. "And I make sure they can count me. But the real reason I'm good at what I do is that when I make an important presentation, I always"—and here his voice dropped to a whisper—"wear expensive underwear."

Another good friend who is a successful advertising executive buys a new tie for a presentation that counts. "When I do that," he says, "I know I count too."

On the day of your presentation, pamper yourself with a facial, a shoeshine, breakfast in bed, or whatever else makes you feel terrific. You're the star of this performance, so treat yourself like one. When you "wear expensive underwear," you're acting as though you deserve the best. That boost to your confidence will carry over into your performance, and you'll end up doing your best. It's practically guaranteed.

Forget the Beauty Myth

I don't subscribe to the misguided idea that you have to turn yourself into one of those "beautiful people" who are continually being held up to us in books and magazines as the ideal to which we should devote all our energies, and without which we're doomed to failure. This chapter isn't about becoming beautiful, with all the ego-centered preoccupation with self that accompanies it. But it is about looking good. About creating a pleasant visual picture for the audience that doesn't confound them with distracting messages. And, at the same time, about freeing you from worry over how your appearance is coming across.

Looking good means your eyes sparkle and you glow with health. It means you carry yourself with pride and move with energy and enthusiasm. When you look good, you dress in a way that's appropriate for your profession and shows respect for your audience. You pay careful attention to detail and are impeccably groomed. Ultimately looking good means you can actually forget about how you look and go back to concentrating on your audience, which is what you've been after all along.

V

Making Magic Happen

12

You Can't Write a Speech

It takes three weeks to prepare a good ad lib speech.
—Mark Twain

When you're asked to prepare a presentation, what's the first step? If you're like most people, you sit down with pen and legal pad, or in front of your computer screen, and diligently begin to write out your speech. There's only one problem. You can't write a speech.

That doesn't mean that I'm advising you to get up there and "wing it," because careful preparation is crucial to your success. But before you put pen to paper, you've got a lot of organizing to do.

At first, this method of speech "writing" may seem painfully methodical, but bear with it. The final product will be clear, concise notes you can use to carry on a wonderfully personal, spontaneous conversation with your audience. If you're new to speechmaking or haven't felt comfortable with your old ways of organizing a presentation, I suggest you work through this process with me in its entirety. Later on you can take some shortcuts.

Step 1. Meeting Audience Needs

Begin your preparation by learning all you can about your audience. Ask yourself questions like:

Who are these people? Why is this subject important to them? If you make the effort to understand your listeners and touch on their concerns, you'll find it much easier to hold their attention.

How knowledgeable are they about your subject? Do they already speak your language or do they require definitions and descriptions? Do they know what questions to ask, or do you have to spoon-feed them the information?

How will they feel about what they're going to hear? If your audience is with you, your job will be much easier. If they're not going to like what you have to say, you'll have to find ways to diffuse a potentially hostile situation. See Chapter 15 on how to respond to a hostile audience.

What's the size of the audience? In the early Voice-Pro days, I was called upon to make a pitch to a potential client. The initial call went something like this: "Come on down to the office, I'll ask someone else to join us, and we can get all our questions answered at the same time." The picture in my mind was of three of us sitting around a corner table, drinking coffee and shooting the breeze. An easy sell, I thought. I arrived at the prospect's office, met my contact, and together we walked to the end of the hall where she threw open a set of double doors.

There they were, thirty executives sitting in the boardroom around the longest table I've ever seen. My contact smiled brightly as she introduced me: "Here is Carolyn Dickson to give us her presentation about Voice-Pro." Gulp! Instead of a pleasant chat around the coffee table, I was expected to deliver a formal presentation to a group of key decision-makers. Fortunately, I knew my subject thoroughly. Neutral Position, centering, and good breathing got me through, and eventually the company became a good client. But my discomfort during that initial interview could have been avoided. I would have saved myself some bad moments had I asked one simple question in advance: "How many people will be there?"

What are the demographics of this group? Often the age, race, sex, and education level of your audience will affect the way you prepare.

Will there be a key decision maker in this audience? If so, how can you reach that person without neglecting the rest of the group?

Step 2. Choosing Your Objective

Once you know who your audience is, decide what you want them to do as a result of your speech. Many business speakers make the mistake of talking only to inform. But all good presentations are inherently persuasive, and the more action-oriented your objective, the more likely you are to make things happen. The objective of a speech must be action-oriented, and it must contain an action verb. *"Use* this information...." *"Tell* your staff...." "Please *support* the project and cooperate with...." *"Give* now." *"Make your decision* quickly." *"Think* about this carefully."

You get an added benefit when your objective is clear. Your speech becomes much more interesting because action words add life. If you don't tell your audience you want them to do something, you're missing a good opportunity to clarify their reasons for listening to you and, in general, to enliven your speech.

Step 3. Determining Your Throughline

We've all heard poorly prepared speakers who begin with one thought and finish up talking about something entirely different. Lloyd George once told the young Winston Churchill, "Don't deliver an essay with so many points. No one can absorb it. Just say one thing." It was good advice, which Churchill heeded in all his great speeches.

Your throughline is your theme, or thesis statement. Like an arrow, it's the thought that guides you directly from your first word to your final "thank you." One client called it the "critical path" that keeps him on track. When your throughline is clear, your audience will be able to sum up your entire presentation in one sentence.

Your throughline is influenced by your objective, but is quite different from it. For example, if I'm talking to a group of smokers, my objective might be: "I hope you will *decide right now* to quit smoking." I can choose from a number of possible throughlines. One possibility is: If you stop smoking, the world of health will open up to you. If I make this choice, I have established a positive tone. All my examples will be motivational stories of people who became healthier because they quit smoking. I will cite statistics that back up my theme of good health. My speech will be positive and upbeat, encouraging people to reach out for a better life.

I might, however, choose another throughline: Smoking is suicide. Here the emotional tone has changed. Instead of motivating them through positive means, I'm scaring my listeners to action. My stories and statistics will reinforce this more negative theme. My objective is the same, but the new throughline changes the entire complexion of my speech.

If you're having trouble getting a handle on your presentation—if it just doesn't seem to "hang together"—go back and make sure your throughline is clear. Ask yourself, "Exactly what am I trying to say here?"

Sometimes your throughline will be clear in your mind from the beginning. Sometimes your objective will come first, and sometimes your audience analysis will influence your choice of both. The order of these steps isn't as important as the fact that all three must be considered before you go on to anything else.

Step 4. Choosing Your Chunks

What are the points you want to make in your presentation? These points are your "chunks," the raw materials or building blocks, of your speech. The number of chunks will vary with your presentation's length. I find that one chunk is often enough for a five minute talk. For a speech of 15 to 20 minutes, three chunks usually provides a nice balance. If you're giving a lengthy presentation, it's wise to think deeper, not broader. Rather than cover more ground by adding additional chunks, beef up the ones you have.

There are a number of ways to put your chunks in order. You can arrange them randomly, put them in chronological order, or create a problem/cause/solution format, to name three.

Proposals, both written and spoken, often use the problem-cause-solution order of chunks. I recently helped a client reorganize her presentation this way. Her speech title was, "The Trouble With Advertising," and the trouble with her presentation was that her examples of good and bad advertising were mixed together. Her audience couldn't tell the difference. Her speech was much better when she reordered her presentation so that Chunk One was filled with examples of poor advertising, Chunk Two described an agency's struggles to turn out quality work, and Chunk Three showed the revised, more effective ads.

Now fill your chunks with support material—study results, statistics, anecdotes, and examples. Keep in mind that stories, examples, illustrations, metaphors, and analogies generate feelings and emotional reactions, while statistics, data, testimonials, and quotations appeal to belief and logical thought. A well-crafted presentation contains a combination of these, appealing to both the logical and emotional sides of the audience. As you work, make sure that each piece of support material connects directly to your throughline.

If your chunks are well organized, you can easily change the length of your presentation. If you suddenly discover that your 20-minute talk must be squeezed into a five-minute slot, you can cut out a chunk or two, or make them all smaller by eliminating part of the support material. On the other hand, you can expand an hour's presentation into a two-day seminar by adding demonstrations and group activities to the same chunks.

Use 3"x 5" cards to keep track of your ideas. Write the main point of each chunk on a card. Each piece of support material then goes on a separate card. As you organize, you can rearrange the cards until you're satisfied with the way your message flows. It's almost like playing solitaire. You'll watch your speech build itself as the cards pile up, and when you're finished, you will have created a strong, well-structured body for your speech, without writing so much as a sentence on your legal pad.

Step 5. Talking It Through

With this homework completed, it's time to get something on paper. But remember, you can't write a speech. First, talk it through. This is the step that turns your piles of facts and stories into a personal, conversational narrative.

Depending on your preference, sit down with pen and paper, your PC, or a tape recorder. Beginning with Chunk 1, start talking, one sentence at a time. Think about what you want to say and then say it—out loud. Let the words go directly from your mouth to your paper, bypassing your inner judges. Talk to the wall; talk to an imaginary person; talk to the dog. Record what you say, exactly the way you say it. Is it conversational? Does it sound like you? This process may feel awkward at first, but it works.

When you've talked and transcribed your way through all your chunks, go back and tighten them up. Eliminate the unnecessary repetition your first-time "talk-through" is bound to produce. Then talk it through again, making sure your throughline and the point of each chunk is clear. If it's necessary, rearrange paragraphs to get the flow just right, and add transitions to carry you gracefully from chunk to chunk. But don't change the conversational tone or your own personal words that make this speech sound just like you. You now have a well-written body for your presentation.

Step 6. Completing Your Manuscript

Now you're ready to add a beginning and an end to your speech. Your audience will decide within a few seconds whether you're worth listening to or not, so you need a strong opening that will connect you with them right off the bat.

Put your throughline and objective right up front. Many speakers like to start slowly and build one idea upon another to a climax where—*voila!*—the overall theme is finally unveiled. This is a mistake. Business audiences are made up of busy people who need to know why they're the recipients of the information you are offering. Every word of your intro should establish that *why*.

I recently talked to a group of former corporate executives on the pros and cons of becoming an entrepreneur. Since these people were all in their late forties and early fifties, I began this way:

> "I'm going to tell you something I've never told another audience. I'm 55 years old. I founded my business when I was 47, and every day since then has been an adventure. It's been the best of times and the worst of times. And I hope you will think carefully about both the upside and the downside of my experience as you make your own decision about whether or not to go into business for yourself."

In this introduction, both my throughline ("every day is an adventure") and my objective ("consider both sides carefully") were clear. And by admitting my own age, I established a strong bond with this particular audience. A good beginning sets the stage. You can relate an anecdote, tell a humorous story, or hit them with a statistic. Whatever your choice of beginnings, it should establish rapport with your audience and give them time to settle down and get focused. At the same time it should, like the straight arrow, propel all of you into the body of your speech.

The end of your presentation is a wrap-up. A good ending provides a *brief* reminder of the points you've covered and states your throughline and objective one more time. There are innumerable ways to close a speech—another story, a quote, a final piece of startling data—but you must make sure the audience is clearly aware of the action you want them to take.

It's perfectly all right to use the words: "In summary...," "In conclusion...," "I'd like to close by..." These words alert the audience that you're approaching the finish line. Too many speakers introduce new material into their summaries, just when their listeners are folding up their tents to go home. In fairness to them, make sure that when you announce your conclusion, you actually conclude.

Step 7. Making an Outline

You're not finished yet. Now that your manuscript is complete, with your words chosen to meet the needs of your audience, reduce it to the leanest possible outline. There are times when you must read a manuscript verbatim, as when specific wording is required for legal purposes. But for most business situations it's better to work from notes. I refer to these notes as a "key-word" or "skeletal" outline.

Put your outline on 8-1/2" x 11" paper. Rather than cramming small cards with lots of information in very small print, use full-sized paper, double spacing, and large print to list single words and phrases. Separate your chunks with white space, so when you look down, your eyes will alight on small blocks of words instead of crowded paragraphs. To further ensure that your eyes will fall where you want them to, use different colored markers to highlight key ideas. Your notes will be even easier to read if you write them on the top two-thirds of your paper and leave the bottom third blank.

Be sure to number your pages. I once witnessed a speaker who fell apart completely, not because he dropped his notes, but because he couldn't get them back in order again.

When you become comfortable with this process of organizing a presentation, you'll find that it really is a quick and easy method of preparation. Your words are the foundation of your presentation, and without them there would be no need for you to speak at all. You can't *write* a speech, but you can *create* one that contains a powerful message and says exactly what you want to say.

13

The Power of Words

I am a Bear of Very Little Brain and long words bother me.
—Winnie-the-Pooh

When you're sitting in an audience, what makes you latch onto and remember certain statements, while most of what the speaker says goes in one ear and out the other? Which words grab and hold your interest, and which ones slide by? Chances are you won't go around the office repeating the pedantic, "Procrastination in the initial planning stages is likely to result in a decline in first quarter revenues." But from the time you first heard it, you've never forgotten the short and punchy adage, "Time is money," which says the same thing.

The words you choose for your presentation should strengthen your message and make it memorable. If your subject is first quarter revenues, then of course you'll have to let everyone know what you're talking about. But you don't have to sound stilted and pretentious while you do it. The most powerful words you can use are clear and precise and cut straight to the heart of the matter. The right word can bring a flash of understanding, while the wrong one can confuse, alienate, or intimidate an audience. It might even turn them off altogether.

Use Small Words

It's not uncommon for business speakers to try to impress their audiences with florid, overblown language. Somehow they feel that if they extend a word and make it longer, they will sound smarter. Not true.

Churchill said, "Short words are best and the old words when short are best of all." The small words of our language have great staying power because they are clear, precise, and strong. Speech that is sprinkled with words like *facilitate, utilize,* and *indicate* is ambiguous. If you say, "She indicated that sales would be off," it's not clear what "she" meant. Did she tell you sales would be off? Did she hint at it? Did she *predict* that sales would be off? One meaning of indicate is to point out, so if that's what you mean, say, "She pointed out that sales would be off." Your sentence is now much stronger.

There's another reason for avoiding large words. They're often cumbersome and difficult to pronounce. If you speak the words of your presentation out loud before you write them down, you'll quickly eliminate the tongue twisters, and the smaller, more conversational words you put in their place will roll easily off your tongue, bringing cadence and rhythm to your speaking.

Keep Your Sentences Short, Too

A government economist who had been criticized for rambling came to me for help in making his speeches more clear and concise. When he delivered his prepared speech for me, we discovered that his opening sentence contained 65 words. I commented that it seemed "just a bit long-winded," and he astonished me by saying, "I'm supposed to be long-winded. I work for the government."

Like multi-syllable words, long sentences are hard to say and even harder to follow. Your listeners, even if they do work for the government, are busy, intelligent people who appreciate clarity. You can help them by chopping up long, convoluted sentences into shorter, simpler ones. In the words of my writer friend, "The period is the noblest punctuation mark of them all. Don't be afraid to use it."

Speak in Active Instead of Passive Voice

Active voice puts subject, verb, and object in that order. "The girl threw the ball!" When you turn the order around, "The ball was thrown by the girl," you've changed the sentence into passive voice, because now the subject, *the ball,* is being acted upon rather than initiating the action. When speakers make excessive use of passive voice, the pictures they paint for the audience are dry and uninteresting. Take, for example, the statement, *"The recommendations were sent on Friday."* What "recommendations"? Who was responsible for them? Where is the action? At best we picture a piece of paper fluttering aimlessly down the hall. The statement becomes more alive when you say, "On Friday, the president recommended..." In this case we can more easily visualize the president, a real person in our eyes, actually doing something.

Whenever you can, give your audience pictures of real people in real situations doing real things. Your presentation will be a stronger and more dynamic one if you speak in active voice whenever you can.

Beware of Jargon and Buzzwords

Jargon is a shorthand language that develops within a particular specialty or profession so the specialists can speak to each other quickly and easily about complex things. Jargon is a valuable tool for communication within a workgroup or task force, but problems arise when you use this "clubhouse" language outside of the club.

According to a recent article in the New York Times, "'Computerese' is one of the more unwelcome side effects of our technological society.... Industry executives, trained to think all day in highly technical, even cosmic terms, talk the way they think. The trouble is that the rest of the world thinks and talks at precomputer levels." It's not only in the computer industry where this happens.

People in technical specialties sometimes use jargon as a status symbol, which is the quickest way I know to alienate an audience. Even if it's not intentional, people feel resentful when they feel they're being patronized and deliberately shut out of the discussion.

When a jargon word becomes trendy, it turns into a buzzword. Like hemlines, buzzwords go in and out of fashion, and while they're in style, they are overused, sometimes to the point of absurdity. A speech laden with buzzwords is a sign of lazy thinking. You can better serve your audience by coming up with the "right" word, not just the one that's fashionable at the moment. It makes sense to recognize buzzwords, understand where they came from, and even use them occasionally, but if you latch onto every buzzword that comes along, you'll call attention to your own lack of originality.

Beware of Value-Laden Words

Many of the words we speak carry with them a great deal of emotional baggage. These value-laden words have an inherent positive or negative connotation. *Justice, commitment, freedom, misguided, permissive,* and *superficial* are a few examples. Political speeches and editorials are often loaded with these value-laden words because they push emotional hot buttons.

While they are legitimate tools of persuasion, value-laden words can also send up red flags. Audiences know when they're being manipulated, so concentrate on using words and images that express your ideas clearly rather than ones that are strictly intended to generate an emotional reaction.

Use Quotes Judiciously

Speakers tend to overuse quotations. It's unnecessary to turn to "Bartlett's Book of Familiar Quotations" every time you're asked to speak, but every once in a while you'll come across a gem that says just exactly what you want to say. In that case, go ahead and use it. Instead of always looking for someone else's words, however, concentrate on expressing yourself in a way that will cause others to want to quote you.

I like quotations. They illustrate that some things were just as true decades or even centuries ago as they are today. But like every other aspect of your presentation, a quote should be used because it reinforces *your* message. For it to be effective, its meaning and the reason you've included it must be instantaneously clear to the audience, so don't use a quotation if it must be explained.

Add a Light Touch

Should you use humor in your presentations? Of course. Humor keeps the audience alert and is a welcome addition to the facts and figures of almost any business presentation. But that doesn't necessarily mean that you should tell a joke. Jokes build to a punchline, setting the speaker up for an uncomfortable moment if the joke falls flat. Skilled joketelling requires excellent timing. It's said that when Oscar Wilde lay dying, a friend asked him what it felt like. "Dying's easy," said Wilde. *"Comedy* is hard."

Unless you're very comfortable with joke-telling, you're better off relating a true story or anecdote that doesn't beg for a belly laugh. If your story causes your listeners to chuckle or perhaps shake their heads and smile, you can give yourself a mental pat on the back and continue. If they don't laugh, you can proceed smoothly and without embarrassment, as if you'd meant to be serious all the time.

Don't tell an ethnic joke or a story based on bias or stereotype, unless you're a member of the group you're talking about. Only a lawyer can get away with telling a lawyer joke. Audiences are sensitive, so laugh at yourself, not at them.

The litmus test for humor in a speech is whether it can be logically connected to your throughline. No matter how funny your story, if it's unrelated to your message, discard it. I think it's a mistake for a speaker to deliver two or three preliminary jokes just to "warm up" the audience. Most of the people I've asked say that, although they laugh dutifully, they're uncomfortable with warm-up jokes and think they're a waste of time. They also easily recognize a joke that may have been originally intended for a group of economists, then altered to fit an audience of attorneys, politicians, or Rotarians. It may have been funny once, but second or third-hand, a joke like this loses its punch.

Humor occurs naturally as a result of living. Be alert for the funny things that happen to all of us. Keep a file of stories from newspapers and magazines that make you laugh, and if one fits, use it to lighten up your presentation.

14

Visual Aids

The basic requirement of professional magic is that you must always know exactly what you are going to do next...and you arrange everything so that you can follow this order without fumbling or confusion."
—From "The Amateur Magician's Handbook"

Knowing how to use visual aids is an important part of your speaking bag of tricks. Like the magician, you're the stage manager as well as the star. It's your job to have the right equipment on hand and pull the rabbit out of the hat without bungling the trick. But unlike the magician, who uses props to create an illusion, your props must reinforce a very real message.

Visual aids illustrate your presentation. They give the audience a clear picture of what you're talking about. A good visual provides the "aha" factor that enables the listener to understand and *remember* the message. It serves the same purpose as when you say, "Here, let me show you," and grab a dinner napkin to draw a quick example. The basic rule for a good visual is: the simpler and more graphic the better.

While visual aids occupy an undisputed place in almost every corporate culture, there's an almost unanimous feeling that much could be done to improve their effectiveness. This means using the right visual at the right time for the right reason, making sure it says no more than what is needed, and handling both it and the equipment that goes with it without fumbling or confusion.

Don't use visuals just because everyone else does. Or to get your outline up where you can see it. Or because when you're fiddling with the equipment you don't have to look at the audience. These are not good reasons. Visuals are meant to be a benefit to the audience and not a crutch for the speaker. So take some time to analyze the visuals you normally use. Put one up on the screen, then go stand in the back of the room and look at it with a fresh eye. Is it clear? Does it have punch and pizzazz? Will it make people say, "Aha! Now I've got it"?

Many speakers skip the critical steps for organizing their spoken material and jump immediately to the question, "What visuals will I need?" When you do this, you're in danger of becoming the anonymous narrator of a slide show. Instead, plan what you want to say, get it organized, and outline it. Then, and only then, make your decisions about where you need visual emphasis and graphic illustration.

Good Visuals Are Clear

The best visuals clarify one point at a time. The simpler, the better—always. Pictures are better than words, and words are better than numbers. Keep it graphic—no sentences and no long tables full of numbers. When you're putting a visual presentation together, try the unexpected. Instead of traditional slides and overheads, think about using freehand drawings, headlines, and cartoons to stimulate interest.

A good visual is always clearly visible to the audience. Viewers shouldn't have to squint or squirm in their seats in order to see. So if you think you're going to have to say, "You may not be able to see this in the back of the room, so I'll read it to you," don't use it. Take the time for a preview trip to the back row to see exactly what the audience will see, and you'll go a long way toward eliminating fuzzy, typewritten pages displayed one after the other on an overhead projector.

The Focus Is Still On You

Remember that you're still the star of this show, so don't let your visuals upstage you. Speak with more volume than normal to compensate for equipment noise. Match the intensity of the visual with your own energy. This is especially important when the audience must turn its attention from slides or a video displayed on a large screen back to your live performance. The psychological letdown can be significant for them, so breathe, Plunge, and project both physically and vocally.

Because the focus of attention should stay on you as much as possible, stand close to the screen so you're always visible, at least peripherally. For the same reason, keep the lights on even while you're explaining what's on the slide or overhead. People will still be able to see even if the picture isn't quite as bright, and it's better to sacrifice some clarity on the screen than lose the connection with your audience.

It's up to you to communicate to the audience where they should look. So bring out your visual when you're ready for them to see it and put it away when it's time for them to turn their attention elsewhere. It's not necessary to space visuals evenly throughout a presentation. If they're needed in only one place, put them there. Then turn off the projector, cover your charts, and move on.

When Things Go Wrong

It can sometimes be hilarious listening to experienced speakers tell tales of visual aid disasters. Bulbs blow up, electricity gets knocked out, pointers get caught in sweaters, and when no one is looking, little gremlins get in the boxes and turn every other slide upside down. So remember that "what can go wrong will go wrong," especially with electronic equipment, and plan accordingly. Bring extra adaptors, extension cords, light bulbs, and any other equipment you might need. And even more important, if something goes wrong and you can't easily correct it, *be prepared to go on without it.*

Your verbal presentation and your visual one should each be able to stand alone, so the audience can understand one without benefit of the other. Adhering to this policy will ensure that your visuals can be clearly understood just by looking at them. It will also allow you to continue speaking if for some reason your visuals aren't available. I once watched two skaters finish their Olympic routine in dead silence after the sound system broke down. They didn't miss a step, and when they were finished, the crowd gave them a standing ovation. You'll win accolades from your audience too when you carry on as if nothing has happened when your microphone goes out, the projector breaks, or the airlines lose your charts and handouts.

Practice, Practice, Practice

You can't get enough practice. The only way to become really comfortable with props is to work with them until they become a part of you. It's not easy to handle the logistical side of a technical presentation and at the same time carry on a relaxed conversation with your audience. It's a little like patting your head and rubbing your stomach at the same time, and it takes just as much coordination.

That's why the few minutes you spend checking out the equipment, learning where the light switches and outlets are, and making sure everything is in order are so important. On the following pages you'll find an evaluation of the different types of visual aids, why they work and why they don't, as well as tips for using them effectively. Use these guidelines to determine which ones are right for your presentation and which ones you can do without.

Incidentally, computer technology is providing extremely sophisticated methods for creating slides and overheads. Dramatic effects can be achieved with "speed dissolve," sound, animation, and other multi-media systems. Detailed discussion of these systems isn't included here because, while complicated visual productions can be exciting, they require the kind of preparation that few business presenters have the time or expertise to accomplish on their own. There's also the danger of being accused of preferring style over substance, when the sophistication of the visual production exceeds the perceived importance of the presentation.

Remember: You are the star of the show, and the basic principles for good visuals always apply, no matter how grandiose the production becomes.

Types of Visual Aids

Flipcharts. Flipcharts are among the most frequently used visual aids. They're typically used with small groups, especially during informal work sessions.

Advantages:
- They focus everyone's attention on the task at hand.
- They help summarize the group's progress and create a "group vision."
- Pages can be torn off and taped on the wall so information remains visible to the group.
- Their informality generates discussion.

Disadvantages:
- They're difficult to carry and store.
- They're not good with large groups.
- Your back will be to the audience as you write, perhaps for extended periods of time.

Tips:

- Use water-based markers. They don't bleed as much and the fumes aren't as bad.
- Use dark colors.
- Use key words and write big. Check the size of your writing from the back of the room.
- If you need to refer back, tab the sheets with masking tape, or tear them off and tape them to the wall.
- Spelling doesn't count when you're working with a flipchart, so don't worry about it.

Overhead Transparencies. Overheads are popular for business presentations because they offer a simple, inexpensive, yet versatile way to illustrate ideas. Most offices keep a supply of blank transparencies on hand, or you can purchase them at any office supply store.

Advantages:

- They're easy to make, easy to use, and easy to file for future use.
- They're ideal for small groups.
- You don't have to turn your back to your audience to use them.
- You don't need a completely darkened room to use the projector.
- You can write on them, creating visuals as you talk.

Disadvantages:

- The "periscope" of the projector can interfere with audience sight lines.
- Glare from the projector can be annoying to both audience and speaker.

Tips:

- Create overheads specifically for your presentation. Don't copy pages directly out of a book.
- Mounting transparencies on cardboard frames will make them easier to handle. You can also make notes on the frames.
- Make them neat and easy to read by using a ruler and large print.

- Color adds interest if it's not overused.
- Build interest with overlays instead of covering words with blank paper.
- Number the frames to keep them in order.
- If you feel the need to apologize for your overheads in any way, don't use them.
- Don't stand right in front of the projector. Your body just doesn't make a very good screen.

35 MM Slides. Most of the guidelines for effective use of overhead transparencies also apply to slides. Slides are best for use with large groups and during formal presentations. They can show off elaborate and complex graphics, or be quite simple and elegant. Most large companies have audio-visual departments that will produce slides for you. You can also work with visual consultants; but remember, consultants are in the business of selling slides, so you could easily end up with many more slides than you really need.

Advantages:

- Slides projected onto a large screen offer a powerful visual image.
- They're suitable for large groups.
- Any good photograph makes a good slide so their versatility is unlimited.

Disadvantages:

- Dark rooms put people to sleep.
- It's easy to lose communication with the audience, because there's no way to maintain a visual connection.
- Good slides can be expensive. "Overkill" with slides is easy.

Tips:

- Put only one idea on a slide. Use bullets instead of sentences.
- Keep as much light in the room as you can, so you don't lose eye contact.
- Talk to the audience, not to the slide.
- Practice using the remote control so slide changes are smooth.
- Use more physical energy than normal to compensate for the darkened room.

- Number the slides and make sure the "slide gremlins" haven't mixed them up or turned them upside down.

Videotapes. Videotapes have replaced film in almost all business presentations, because they're easier to handle and the tapes don't break as often. You can pause for explanations or replay portions of a program. Videotapes offer excellent visual impact. They add variety to long presentations and work well for groups of all sizes.

Tips:

- Make sure monitors are large enough to be seen by all.
- Know how to operate all equipment and test it ahead of time.

Handouts. Develop your handout as a reference piece for use by the audience after your presentation. Be sure it stands alone and doesn't require personal explanation in order to be understood. If possible, save handouts and pass them out at the end of the session, because people like to read ahead and you may lose their attention. If you do distribute handout pieces during your presentation, it's up to you to control their use. Tell your listeners when to read along with you and when to put the material aside.

The deadliest business presentations are those where the speaker duplicates handout pages, flashes them on a screen, and then reads the screen while the audience follows along in the handout. The only possible rationale for this kind of a presentation is that it requires absolutely no preparation or effort by the speaker. It's torture for the audience, however, so don't do it.

Three Dimensional Models. Nothing hits home like the real thing. Models work especially well to display the concept of a new building or remodeling, or to unveil a new product.

You'll never find anything that works better or describes a process more clearly than the object itself.

Advantages:

- They offer great visual impact.
- You can use normal room lighting
- Models are independent of the speaker and normally don't have mechanical controls.

Disadvantages:
- They draw attention away from speaker.
- They're time consuming to make and often expensive.

Tips:
- Check all working parts before the presentation.
- Have the model on view before and after your presentation.
- Don't pass it around or encourage viewing while you're speaking.

VI

The Performance Wizard

15

Preparing For Performance

A nail is driven out by another nail; habit is overcome by habit.
　　　　　　　　　　　　　　　—Erasmus

The best athletes know that training doesn't start the moment they enter the locker room or set foot on the field. Posture, breathing, mental outlook, nutrition, sleeping habits, and many of the other aspects of daily life affect their performance both on and off the field. Real excellence in speaking also requires a long-term commitment.

A little deep breathing a few minutes before your presentation may help to calm your jitters, but it's no substitute for sustained effort over a lifetime.

During performance, you won't have time to think about making the right gesture or pronouncing the t's at the ends of your words because you'll be busy thinking about your audience and the message you have for them. Your technique must be automatic, and over time the continual practice of the exercises in this book will make it so.

But rehearsal, or preparing for a given performance, is very different from practice, which is the repetition of technical exercises. A rehearsal is an actual runthrough of what you plan to say and do, preferably in the space where you're going to be speaking. Rehearsal is a critical step in preparing for performance. I'm often called in to coach speakers during rehearsal, and I find that the best performers take this process very seriously. Ideally, a rehearsal approximates your real performance as closely as possible.

Rehearsing Effectively

During rehearsal, decide where you're going to stand and actually get up out of your seat and walk there. Take a few minutes to look out at your imaginary audience, put faces on them, and start thinking about them as real people. Then speak to your audience, using the first few sentences of your presentation. Get used to the way your voice sounds in the room and how it feels to project in that space.

Rehearsal is the time to discard your manuscript and work with an outline or a few key words. Your initial runthroughs will probably feel awkward because, when you're working with an outline for the first time, your words don't always come out in just the right way. But after a few rehearsals, you'll come to know your speech very well. As you rehearse, you'll find your speech won't be identical every time. New words will come to you, and your presentation will grow and change each time you give it. Make sure you avoid the temptation to memorize your lines. If you commit a speech to memory and recite it verbatim, it will sound mechanical.

Use your rehearsal time to experiment with movements and gestures, letting the flow of your words dictate your movements. Walk out to greet the audience, then back to the projector, then over to the screen to point for emphasis. Repeat these actions over and over again till they feel comfortable. Find out what it feels like to lean conversationally against the podium or to sit on the edge of the table. Does the action fit your message? If it does and it feels right to you, use it during performance.

Rehearsal is also the time to check your props and visual aids, making sure that all your equipment is working. If your presentation is a formal one that demands the use of a podium, take some rehearsal time to get used to it. See how it feels when your hands rest quietly on the sides of the podium, and when you gesture, keep your hands high so they're visible. Because a podium places a physical barrier between you and your audience, you'll need to increase your energy level a degree or two. So give an extra push on the Plunger to make sure you're projecting.

If you'll be using a microphone, now's the time to practice with it. If the mike is mounted on the podium, position it so it's a few inches away from your mouth. A microphone isn't meant to be a substitute for projection, so float your head, speak with energy, and let the mike amplify the sound of your voice, not take over entirely. Besides, when your mouth is too close to the mike, your *p's* and *t's* will "pop" and your breath will sound like you're speaking through a wind tunnel. If you're wearing a lapel mike that drags a long cord behind it, practice walking around so you won't trip. The trick to working with a mike is to become so familiar with it that you're able to forget about it.

Knowing how to rehearse effectively is one of the tricks that separates amateur from professional performers. Not many business people recognize its importance, and even those who do often feel uncomfortable about talking to an audience that isn't there. Remember that no professional performer would dream of setting foot on stage without adequate rehearsal, and it's never foolish to be well prepared. Focus your thoughts, center yourself, and treat rehearsal as an integral part of the performance itself. It will be time very well spent.

Mental Rehearsal

When I rehearse, I find it helpful to spend a few moments sitting alone in the audience. I look up at the platform and imagine myself beginning my presentation. I ask, "How would I want to see myself if I were in the audience?" Then I see myself performing in just that way. I watch and listen to myself, visualizing the strength, the confidence, and the humor I will display up there.

There is a great deal of evidence that this kind of visualization, or mental rehearsal, is one of the best ways to improve performance in any activity. Scientists have found that whenever you imagine a physical movement, the nerves that transmit messages from your brain to your body go through their paces, and a subtle corresponding muscular impulse takes place. Through visualizing, you reinforce mental pathways and fine-tune the circuits you'll be using when you go into action. Golfer Jack Nicklaus calls the process of visualization "going to the movies." He says he never hits a shot, not even in practice, without first imagining every detail of it in his mind.

You can use visualization to rehearse your own performances. When you stand at the podium during practice, see your audience in your mind's eye, and mentally cast your net over them. Later, spend some time sitting in the audience and imagine your performance just the way you want it to happen. Nicklaus says that it does him no good to visualize the shot if he doesn't see it going where he wants it to go. So carry your visualization through to the payoff—the audience motivated to action, the satisfied customer, or the inner pleasure of knowing you've done a good job.

Taking Command of the Variables

In addition to preparing yourself for performance, you can also take command of many of the external factors which will play a part in the success of your presentation. Start out by taking a good look at your surroundings.

If you can, check out the room where you'll be speaking well ahead of time. Know where the light switches are, and the electrical outlets. Get used to the lighting and make sure there is enough light so you can easily see your notes.

Make sure your footing is good. The raised platforms set up in hotels and conference centers are seldom very sturdy, and I always like to walk around on them for a few minutes to find out where the wobbles are.

Find out if you can adjust the room temperature yourself or if you must call someone else to do it. In fact, if you will need a technician to perform any services at all, be sure to get acquainted and learn how to reach that person quickly if it becomes necessary.

If the audio/visual equipment you're going to use is different from the equipment you rehearsed with, try to find time for another technical runthrough. Try an overhead transparency, or a slide or two, to make sure your visuals can be seen from the back row. If you need table space to lay out your materials, make sure it's there.

A little logistical reconnaissance will go a long way to allaying the natural fears that go with unfamiliar territory, and when the time arrives for you to move into your speaking space, you'll feel like you're coming home.

Rituals and Warm-Ups

For centuries, artists and performers have used personal rituals to help them prepare for a performance. Supposedly Charles Dickens always faced north when he wrote because he thought he could take advantage of the magnetic fields. Today many sports figures use rituals that they think help them compete. These routines may be very elaborate, dictating what they eat for breakfast, whether or not they shave, and how they lace their shoes. No matter how simple or how elaborate, rituals are more than just superstition. They have value because they get people ready for performance by helping them prepare mentally.

Business people seldom have time for extensive mental preparation, no matter how important they agree it is to performing at their best. They rush out of the office and up to the boardroom, or across town in the rain and through traffic to make a sales pitch. But however rushed you feel, the moment you face your audience, you must be centered and focused. A warm-up routine, one that becomes your own personal ritual, will help you to switch gears and focus your mind.

Your warm-up routine can include Shrugs and Shakes, deep breathing, the Plunger and Windbag, centering and visualization—whatever the key exercises are for you. It doesn't have to be long and should be designed so it can be done quickly—right before you leave your office or in the car when you're on your way. Eventually this routine will evolve into one you accomplish mentally—in the hall, in the elevator, or right before you open the boardroom door. It doesn't really matter what you do as long as it is your own personal ritual and works for you.

16

Letting Go

"Do you know why you cannot wait for the shot and why you get out of breath before it has come? The right shot at the right moment does not come because you do not let go of yourself. You do not wait for fulfillment, but brace yourself for failure."

—Eugen Herrigel
Zen in the Art of Archery

Chris sat in the Voice-Pro studio and explained how devastating it would be if her upcoming presentation weren't perfect. "I'm in line for a vice presidency, and I'll be passed over if I show any sign of weakness." As she talked about her fears, her body began to tighten up, and pretty soon her voice and hands were shaking with emotion. Chris was working herself into a state where, no matter how thoroughly she prepared herself, she was bound to fall short of not only her own expectations but everyone else's.

When people are under intense pressure, they tend to fixate on all the things that can possibly go wrong. By intensifying their efforts to avoid disaster, they paradoxically succeed in accomplishing the very thing of which they are afraid. The more involved Chris got in her driving need to give a successful presentation, the less likely she was to do a good job.

The final step in preparing for performance, after you've practiced and prepared and rehearsed to the best of your ability, is to "let go." Letting go can best be described as *"allowing* something to happen instead of *making* it happen." The concept of letting go is inherent in Zen Buddhism. The words of Zen master S. T. Suzuki capture its meaning: "Great works are done when (one) is not thinking." Many psychologists teach letting go techniques to their patients as a supplement to therapy, and organizations such as Alcoholics Anonymous incorporate it into their 12-step programs for overcoming addictions. It's a proven method for releasing people from overdrive and anxiety.

Letting go is very different from being "laid back" and has nothing at all to do with "winging it." The technique allows you to hold onto your constructive goals, while at the same time it releases you from a counter-productive, over-involved, debilitating need to achieve these goals. Letting go takes the pressure off. It's been called a form of "mental judo," which, like centering, leaves you calm, steady, and balanced.

Athletes search endlessly for ways to let go during competition. They talk about, "playing dumb," or "going on automatic pilot," or "giving yourself up to the game." They feel that "thinking is what gets you caught from behind," and "if you're not thinking about anything, hopefully you're thinking about everything."

In speaking, the "letting go" technique enables you to release, once and for all, your obsession with ego thoughts and replace them with audience thoughts. You speak well simply because you've released yourself from the need to speak well. You're able to concentrate on what to say rather than on whether or not you're saying it badly. You're freed up to be creative, spontaneous, and expressive.

The Detachment Paradox

Richard, a young advertising executive, recently shared with me some of the thoughts that go through his mind before making a new business pitch. "Everyone's counting on me to get this business. If I don't get it, I'll look like a fool. All the time I've put into it will be wasted. I've got to get them to like me." It's no wonder that, by the time Richard's presentations rolled around, he was a nervous wreck. Like Chris, who was expending all her energy not to jeopardize her vice presidency, Richard was putting tremendous pressure on himself. And in doing so, he was very likely sabotaging his own work.

The detachment paradox says that the more you release yourself from the need to do something, the more likely you are to do that very thing. By removing the pressure to achieve, you'll end up achieving more.

For Chris, understanding the detachment paradox meant that she could give the presentation of her life without paralyzing herself with worries about a promotion over which she had no control. For Richard, it meant giving up preoccupation with his reputation in the agency and turning his energy and enthusiasm to the new client's public relations campaign.

When you detach yourself, you don't give up the goal; you only give up your need to achieve the goal. When you succeed at this, you find, surprisingly enough, that the goal is easier to attain than you ever thought possible. You don't have to try nearly as hard.

Exercises for Letting Go

Like the other techniques in this book, letting go is a skill that must be practiced until it comes naturally to you when you need it. But take it easy. Letting go isn't something you can force. If you tell yourself, "I'm going to accomplish this if it kills me," you'll throw the detachment paradox into reverse and discover that the more you push, the less release you'll feel. So experiment with this technique, play with it, turn it loose, and see what happens.

Letting Go Exercise 1. Even though letting go is a form of mental practice, it's easier to learn by starting with a material object rather than something elusive like thoughts or feelings.

1. Choose a small object that has enough weight to fall to the floor when you drop it. A pen, an eraser, or an orange will do nicely. Ask yourself, "Am I willing to let go of this pen (or whatever) and see it fall?" If you're able to answer "yes" to that question, go on to the next step.
2. Hold the object loosely in your hand and say out loud, "I choose to let go of this pen." As you say the words "let go," loosen your fingers and allow the object to fall. Repeat this several times until your fingers automatically loosen on the words "let go," and the object drops as if by its own volition.
3. Repeat the exercise again in exactly the same way, only without actually holding an object. As you say the words "let go," move your hand in the same releasing gesture as you used when you dropped the object. Repeat this until the symbolic action becomes synonymous in your mind with the dropping of the object.

You may be able to accomplish the feeling of release almost immediately, or it may take you several sessions of practice. But eventually your mind and body will respond to both the verbal "let go" command and the symbolic "let go" gesture.

Letting Go Exercise 2. The next step in learning to let go is to turn your attention to your need rather than the object. Identify something that bothers you but isn't important enough to trigger a severe emotional response on your part. At this moment, I can use the irritating hum of my laptop computer as I write these words. A grease spot on the floor, a slow elevator, a forgotten lunch date are other examples of things you might like to change but aren't of immediate earth-shattering import. For the purposes of this exercise, let's choose the grease spot on the floor as an example.

1. Ask yourself the question, "Am I willing to let go of my irritation over the fact that this rug has a spot on it?" This question zeroes in on the critical issue of your willingness to change. Be honest with yourself, and when you feel you can answer "yes" to this question, go on to the next step.
2. Repeat out loud, "I choose to let go of my irritation over the spot on this floor." Add your symbolic hand gesture as you say the words "let go." You've now released yourself from any over-involved concern about the state of the floor. You can forget about the spot. Or you can acknowledge that the spot is there but not fret over it. Or you can use a good rug shampoo to get rid of it. Letting go allowed you to move beyond the aggravation and deal with the problem in a practical way.
3. Practice letting go of other minor irritations in your life. Gradually, you'll find that just the spoken or unspoken words "let go" will trigger the release, and the situation will look or sound or feel differently to you than it did before. Or the symbolic hand gesture will be enough, and a tiny flick of your finger will do the trick.

Letting Go to Speak

When you're comfortable with using the letting go technique in situations of only minor importance, it's time to put it to use in a speaking situation.

For Chris, letting go meant releasing the anxiety she felt about whether or not she would be promoted to vice president. She first asked herself the "willingness" question. "Am I willing to let go of my concern over this promotion in order to give a good presentation?" It was tough to confront herself with this question, as her need to worry about it was strong, but she was finally able to answer "yes."

Chris then repeated out loud, "I choose to let go of the anxiety I feel over this promotion," using the symbolic hand gesture she had chosen. Because her presentation required a number of rehearsals, she began each session with this letting go statement. Each time she felt a greater sense of release and it was increasingly easier for her to concentrate on her goal of reaching the audience.

Owning Your Goals

When I first introduced the letting go concept to Richard, he did well when practicing with objects, but he found it difficult to detach himself from wanting his presentation to win him a contract. "Of course I want to win," he said. "It's my job to win, it's what I'm paid to do, it's what I'm expected to do, why what if..." and he was off and running.

For Richard, it helped to make a clear distinction between continuing to own your goals, while you let go of the need. It was perfectly reasonable for Richard to want to win the new business; his argument was valid. But the question wasn't whether Richard should give up the goal of providing a good service to the client; the question was: Did Richard choose to let go of his need for winning personal glory and recognition? Could he give up—just for now—the wanting?

When Richard was able to make this distinction, he found it much easier to let go. He realized he wasn't giving up his ability to speak well, he was just giving up his disabling preoccupation with it.

A Matter of Trust

Letting go works best when you trust it will happen. Trust that your preparation, practice, and rehearsal will have made you ready for your performance. Trust that, when you're sitting at the speaker's table, or waiting in the wings to be called to the podium, or readying yourself for your quarterly report to the Board, your instinct and training will take over. That with a tiny symbolic hand gesture or an inaudible whispering of two simple words, you can put yourself on automatic pilot, and you will be a good speaker.

Without effort you'll feel your muscles relax slightly and your breath flow more easily. You may notice your inner monologue has changed and you have a different mental picture of yourself and your audience.

Letting go is the culmination of your study of speaking. It encompasses every principle, every concept, and every exercise and technique that I've talked about in this book. Focus, relaxation, centering, breathing, energy, expression, organization, practice, and rehearsal—all come together and are set in motion by the letting go process. Because speaking is a situation where the stakes are often high and almost everyone has an overwhelming fear of looking foolish, vulnerable, or inept, letting go is a most difficult skill to master. On the other hand, because it needs no force or intensity behind it—because you just do it—it can be the easiest skill to master.

As paradoxes go, it's in a class by itself.

17

It's Showtime

My friend the theatre director is also a fine actor. He says, "When I'm on stage, I never make a mistake. Oh, there may be things I'll work on before my next performance, but when I'm up there, everything I do is absolutely right." When you're on stage and "in the moment" of your performance, you can have this same gift.

From the moment your name is announced, you're in charge. You're the expert, asked to speak because you have information that other people want. Your position as the speaker automatically provides you with all the authority you need, so unless you're addressing an exceptionally hostile audience, your listeners are already in your court.

Establishing Rapport

An audience will decide in the first half-minute or so whether or not a speaker is worth listening to, so your entrance and your opening are extremely important. You can demonstrate that you're in command and willing to assume the authority your position gives you by walking purposefully to where you want to stand, positioning your notes, and pausing for a moment to look at your audience. Take the time to really see them. If they seem to need a moment to settle down, wait. Only when you have their complete attention should you begin to speak.

Use the first few moments of your presentation to establish rapport with your audience. You can do this, first by understanding that they're already yours, and then by showing them that you are committed—to them and to the message you have for them. Of course, this doesn't mean fawning over them or changing the content of your presentation because they may not like what you're going to say. But it does mean making them comfortable by being comfortable with yourself, watching them carefully for feedback, and acknowledging what you see and hear in an open, forthright manner.

A few years ago, I traveled several hundred miles to a conference in order to hear a particular speaker. I could hardly believe my ears when he opened his presentation by saying, "I really haven't had time to prepare my remarks to you this morning, so I jotted down a few notes in the cab coming over from the airport." And like a second-rate Abe Lincoln, he pulled an envelope out of his pocket and started to speak.

Although this speaker's opening remarks were sincere, their only purpose was to make him feel better, so there was no power in them to win over the audience. In fact, by admitting that he hadn't taken the time to prepare for an audience of people who had spent time and money to come hear him, this speaker did a pretty good job of alienating everyone. By initially demonstrating concern for our needs, he would have laid a strong foundation for the rest of his presentation. A good opening captures the attention of your audience, increases your confidence, and propels you into the body of your speech.

Adjusting During Performance

No matter how well prepared you are or how much you've done to manage the variables within your command, you can never be sure that everything will go exactly as planned. Something could go wrong. If you stay centered and keep your sense of humor when the unforeseen occurs, you'll be able to handle it with composure and self-assurance.

Have you ever been to the theatre and watched something happen on the set that wasn't really a part of the play? I once saw an amateur actress accidentally knock over a vase, spilling water and flowers all over the floor. She was obviously startled and unsure of what to do, so she did nothing, continuing with her lines as if the mishap hadn't occurred. At that moment she lost her audience. All eyes went to the bouquet of flowers lying in a puddle on the floor, and they stayed there until the end of the scene, when the water got wiped up and the flowers put back on the table. In real life, if you knock something over, you pick it up and put it back where it belongs. That's what the actress should have done.

If you drop something during a speech, pick it up. If your slide is upside down, turn it over. If there's a distraction in the back of the room, acknowledge it. You can be sure that if you're distracted by something going on, others will be too. Instead of ignoring the distraction and pretending it's not there, it's better to say, "The fans in this room are noisy. I'll try to speak up and if you have any trouble hearing me, let me know."

Often an unexpected occurrence that disrupts a performance can be the very thing that brings you and the audience together. I once gave a dinner speech in a restaurant with what I am convinced was a cardboard divider between two banquet rooms. On my side, I was talking to a group of independent auditors about giving effective presentations, and on the other side a birthday party was taking place, complete with popping balloons, hoots of laughter, and a polka band. There was absolutely nothing I could do to control the noise, and my getting upset about it would only have made a bad situation worse, so I decided to make the noise a part of my presentation. I gave a demonstration of the techniques and benefits of voice projection and talked at length about how to handle disturbances without losing your cool. The audience stuck with me, we laughed a lot, and everyone ended up having a great time.

Another time I was able to salvage a potentially disastrous situation just by dealing with it openly. At hotel conferences, people in the audience often wander in and out of the room, and there's not much anyone can do about it. In the middle of one of my presentations, almost a third of the audience got up and left. This is the stuff speakers' nightmares are made of, and no amount of preplanning can prepare you completely for when it happens. I handled this situation by breaking off in mid-sentence and asking, "Am I supposed to be finished now?" One of the "leavers" said, "Oh no, we weren't supposed to be here at all because of a scheduling conflict. But we came anyway because we wanted to hear what you had to say."

Relieved that I wasn't the object of a public protest, I called a short break. Then we went on with the session, and all ended well. But if I had ignored this massive exit, I would have felt terrible, and the people remaining would have sat in uncomfortable silence for as long as we were together in that room.

Overcoming Mistakes

No matter how experienced you are, you will occasionally screw up. Your papers may be out of order, you may lose your train of thought, or you may say, "I'm pleased to be here in Texas," when you're really in Oklahoma. When handled deftly, however, mistakes are quickly forgotten by the audience. In fact, the audience will forgive you almost anything. They'll forgive your stumbling over words. They'll forgive your not knowing all the answers. They'll forgive your falling on your face on your way up the platform steps. What they absolutely will not forgive is your embarrassment over these things when they happen. This is where the ability to laugh at yourself will serve you well.

Pamela is a fundraiser for a large, prestigious hospital and school of medicine. The alumni group to which she was speaking was made up of highly successful doctors, many of whom were skeptical of the need to contribute their hard-earned dollars to support a wealthy school. Pamela was concerned about making a good impression on this tough audience and had worked hard on her opening. When it came time for her to speak, she stood up, looked out over her audience, took a deep breath, cast out her net, and said, "Ladies and gentlemen, in order to spend one year at this university, it will cost a medical student over two thousand dollars!"

"I wanted to fall through the floor when I realized I'd said 'two' instead of 'twenty,'" she said later. "All my hard work went right down the drain with my very first sentence. But then I thought about how preposterous my statement must have sounded to those doctors. So I just laughed and said, 'Well, it may have cost $2,000 when you went to school, but it costs a heck of a lot more now.' Everyone laughed, the ice was broken, and I went on to give a pretty good speech." Pamela raised a great deal of money that evening, in no small part because she was able to overcome an embarrassing flub with humor and style.

Take what you do seriously, but don't take yourself so seriously that you can't laugh at your own mistakes. More times than not, you'll be able to turn them to your advantage.

Fielding Questions

Many speakers find that the question-and-answer period is the most enjoyable part of the presentation. A good presentation stimulates thought, and good questions will move you from a monologue into a discussion format, bringing with it the satisfaction of good conversation. But for inexperienced speakers, Q&A can be something they would rather avoid. A speaker's biggest fear is looking inadequate—of being out of control. If no one asks a question, will you be standing there looking stupid? If someone does ask a question, will you know the answer? And will you be able to think on your feet fast enough to handle the situation, whether questions come or not?

Audience analysis and preliminary planning will help you prepare for Q&A, and as you gain experience in fielding questions, you'll come to enjoy it. Every organization has accepted procedures for Q&A, and you probably have a good sense of the rules already. In an in-house presentation, most questions are informational in nature. They are usually a request for you to elaborate on a point you've already made, or they are "what if" questions that require some speculation on your part. You can prepare yourself by anticipating all possible questions and treating them as chunks, formulating your answers as completely as you have prepared the presentation itself.

If you're invited to speak to an outside organization, you'll need to ask your contact person two questions of your own: 1) "Do you want a question-and-answer session?" and 2) "How many people will be in the audience?" If it's a big group, over a couple of hundred, request that someone on their side be put in charge of audience participation, with a process in place for orderly questioning. If it's a smaller group, it will be easier for you to handle Q&A on your own.

When you're asked a question, repeat it so everyone can hear it. If you're not sure you understand the question, ask that it be explained, or rephrase it in your own words and check back that you're correct. If your answer to the question is short, talk directly to the questioner. If you must elaborate or tell a story to illustrate your point, open up to include the entire audience.

Keep your answers as short as possible, so they don't become speeches in their own right. Sometimes a questioner will want to follow up with an additional question. That's fine, but beware of the person who tries to monopolize the conversation. You can stay in charge by saying, "I see you have further questions, and I'll be happy to stay after the meeting to talk with you. Right now I think it's important that everyone get a chance to speak." Then quickly move on to the next question.

A similar response works well when a question is off the subject. You can say, "That's a good question, but in the interest of time I'd like to limit my comments to this particular area. I'll be happy to stay after the meeting to speak to you personally about that subject."

What if you don't know the answer to a question? Say so. Just because you're speaking, you're not obligated to have the answer to every possible question on the tip of your tongue. If it's evident that you've done your homework, you don't need to apologize or to stumble over a contrived answer. You might say, "I don't know for sure, but my guess is..." Or, "That's out of my area of expertise. Perhaps someone in the audience can help me out." You can also offer to look up the information and forward it to the questioner. In none of these instances will you look inadequate. Instead, the audience will appreciate your candor and your willingness to help.

Individuals, particularly in a large audience, are often reluctant to ask questions. (Their inner judges are at work, too.) Give them time to speak up, and don't worry if the silence seems overwhelming. Your pause will allow them needed thinking time. It's a good idea to have a question or two in the back of your mind, so you can prime the pump. "One question I'm often asked is...?" (If you make your own question a bit controversial, you'll give them tacit permission to ask the tough ones.) Then answer the question as if it really came from someone. Some speakers get the conversation started by planting a question or two ahead of time. Whatever you do, don't embarrass the audience in any way or scold them for not entering into the discussion.

Generally, your listeners will be looking for information when they ask you questions. It's unlikely you'll come up against someone who is deliberately trying to put you on the spot. However, that does happen sometimes. In Chapter 18, we'll talk about handling the tough questions that occur in media interviews. The techniques discussed there will help you deal with the hecklers.

It's A Wrap

Your tale is told and it's time to conclude your remarks. But remember, it's not over till it's over. And it's up to you to let people know that you've finished. I've witnessed many fine presentations that drifted into nothingness because the speaker didn't know how to get off the stage.

Make sure you let people know you're through. A strong conclusion signals to your audience that it's time to applaud, to ask their questions, or to get up and leave. If you're moving from your prepared speech into Q&A, a bridging statement is helpful, like, "This concludes my formal remarks, and we still have a few minutes. Is there anything you'd like to ask?" If there are no questions, and your time is almost up, graciously comment, "Well, it seems we've covered it. Let me leave you with one last thought..." Sum up quickly, thank them, and you're home free.

There are two schools of thought on whether or not to thank the audience. One side feels that you have done the audience a favor, that they are privileged to be there, and that they should be thanking you. The other side takes the position that you should be grateful for their presence and the fact that they are listening to you at all. My own feeling is that these people have given you the honor of their considerate attention, and since you are the person in charge, it's up to you to recognize this courtesy and express your appreciation. A simple thank you at the end of a presentation is, therefore, very appropriate.

When you're finished, gather your notes together quickly and return to your seat with the same purposeful energy you started with. Understand that you're still the center of attention until you leave the room or until the next speaker begins.

18

Credibility: The End Result

To be persuasive we must be believable; to be believable we must be credible; to be credible we must be truthful.
—Edward R. Murrow

I've found that what most people want for themselves whenever they communicate with others is to be seen as credible. The word credibility stems from the Latin *credere*, which means *to believe* or *to entrust*. A credo is a religious statement of beliefs; if something is incredible, it's impossible to believe; and we give credence (belief) to ideas when we accept them as true. When you have credibility, people believe you, believe in you, and are more likely to act on what you say.

The interesting thing about credibility is that, even though you may have it, it's not something that originates within you. Credibility is born in the mind of the beholder; it is *bestowed* upon you by other people. This puts it out of your control, since you can't dictate what goes on in someone else's mind. So credibility ends up being an elusive will-o'-the-wisp that seems to come and go without your ever having it permanently within your grasp.

Research and my own experience have shown me, however, that you can *influence* another person's belief in you when you demonstrate the qualities of integrity, expertise, dynamism, and open mindedness. I say "demonstrate" because your *possession* of these qualities doesn't guarantee your credibility. It's only when your audience recognizes these qualities in you—sees them, hears them, and feels them—that they will deem you credible.

Credibility and Leadership

It's not surprising that the key qualities of credibility and leadership are the same. What are the qualities of a leader? Think about it....

One recognized characteristic of a leader is demonstrated expertise in a particular field. When you examine the credentials of recognized business leaders, as well as those in other fields such as science, medicine and politics, it becomes apparent that these leaders didn't get where they are simply because they had the right connections or were in the right place at the right time. They know what to do, how to do it, and have profited from the experiences of a lifetime. Particularly in business, where competition is keen and expertise is valued and rewarded, people are unlikely to place their trust in anyone who can't back their words with actions.

It's also a fact that as soon as you demonstrate competence in one field, people expect that expertise to carry over into everything you do. That's why athletes tell us what shoes to wear, and other celebrities push coffee, chocolate pudding, and telephone companies. It's why MBA's command high starting salaries, even though they may not have had previous business experience. And it's why your audience expects you—a competent manager, executive, consultant, professional in any field—to speak well whether you've had formal training or not.

Another quality that sets leaders apart is their awareness of their own personal power. This power comes from the same energy source that we speak of when we talk about centering. Leaders are able to tap into this energy source at will, using it to empower themselves and motivate others. For some, this connectedness to a deeper (or higher) power takes on a spiritual dimension. For others, it comes from a strong sense of purpose, of justice, or from a vision for themselves or for a better world.

When I talk to leaders about this power, they often point to integrity as its springboard. Integrity comes from knowing and living by your principles. When you have integrity, you do what you say you will do, when you say you will do it. You are straight with people—honest even when it hurts—and people know they can rely on you to look for the right way to do things, not just the expedient way. When tough decisions must be made, you're able to let your honor and integrity guide you, and it never fails you. Integrity is strengthening and ennobling. Integrity gives you power.

People with personal power display an inner intensity, a silent passion that speaks volumes about their courage, commitment, and determination. It has nothing whatsoever to do with being loud or

pushy. Instead there's a quiet authority about them that other people feel and respond to.

Integrity, expertise, and dynamic intensity are nothing without
the one trait that makes leaders truly loved and accepted. That trait is
humanness, which manifests itself in an openness to the thoughts
and feelings of other people and a willingness to show your own.
This means that you're willing to consider differing points of view,
even though they're in opposition to yours. It also means that while
you can look at situations objectively, without automatic condemna-
tion of the other players, you're willing and able to display your own
capacity for feeling.

Building Credibility

I often introduce the subject of credibility near the beginning of a
presentation, before the audience has a chance to get to know me.
With a mental crossing of my fingers, I ask them what has determined for them in these first few minutes whether or not I'm credible. I hear things like, "you're credible because I can hear you," "you
look at us all the time," "you came out from behind the table," "you
don't hesitate, you just say things," "you don't seem at all nervous,"
"you look like you're enjoying yourself." These people really don't
know anything about me, but they make very strong judgments
about whether or not they believe me, and they make them very
quickly based on how I behave.

Audiences will be making snap judgments about you from the
moment you speak your first word and even before, as you walk into
the room and arrange your materials in preparation for your presentation. They are more than willing to take you at face value. Even
the speaker with high initial credibility born of credentials and past
experience will lose much of that credibility as a result of a poor presentation.

I've been witness to a perfect illustration of this over the years as
I've listened to a certain CEO address large community groups. A bril-
liant, dynamic, civic leader, this CEO has the trust and respect of
everyone who knows him. He often chairs committees whose work
ultimately has a dramatic impact on everyone in his city. One on one
and in small groups he's a master of communication. Yet in a public
forum, he often damages his cause because none of his greatness
shows. He mumbles and shuffles through papers. He hesitates and

seems to forget what he's trying to say. He refuses to look at us. In fact, he's so uncomfortable when he's before a large group of people that it's painful to watch. Belief in him plummets. And his credibility is lost.

Conveying Your Credibility

It's essential that you convey to your audience the qualities that will make you credible in their eyes. Every principle, every activity, and every exercise in this book is designed to help you do just that. For example, your open, erect posture, relaxed manner, and direct gaze will communicate your honesty and integrity, telling people you're being "straight" with them. Your strong voice, with words spoken without hesitation, tells them you know what you're talking about.

When I began coaching speakers at Voice-Pro, I used the Plunger, the Windbag, and the other exercises and techniques of diaphragmatic breathing to build the vocal projection they needed to be easily heard. Then I discovered something. When, after someone had completed a round of exercises, I asked class members what they were hearing, I got more than the expected comments about increased volume. I heard things like: "You're speaking with a lot more authority," "Now I really believe you," and "You sure sound like you know what you're talking about." Dan, a high-ranking executive in the construction industry, felt his personality change as the Plunger exercise activated his diaphragm muscle and his voice boomed; and one of his colleagues announced with pleasure, "Finally, the real Dan just walked in."

Filling the lower third of the lungs with air, using the Plunger, and speaking with diaphragmatic support developed not only the *vocal* projection I was after, but much, much more. My clients were developing projection in every sense of the word. The entire person projected: eyes sparkled, movements and gestures strengthened, voices carried, and they took unchallenged ownership of the space they occupied. Even their skin tone seemed to improve. And their audiences, both in class and back on the job, responded instinctively and positively to the power of that projection. I began to realize that my clients were connecting with the inner sources of their personal power, with magnetism and credibility being the end result. One woman said, "I feel like I know more!" What a wonderful gift she had given herself.

Research in the areas of stress management, mind-body relationships, and biofeedback has revealed new evidence that supports what I suspected—that dynamism, this wonderful combination of energy and power, is directly related to the amount of oxygen being circulated in the blood. The more oxygen, the greater the energy. When you train your body to breathe deeply and speak with diaphragmatic support—not just when you're speaking to an audience, but all the time—you will become vibrant and alive. It's that simple, and every bit as miraculous as it sounds.

A Final Thought

My friend the theatre director once told me, "When you solve an acting problem, you solve a life problem." The same is true as you train yourself to be a credible speaker. When you learn to relax under pressure, to breathe from the diaphragm, to look at and listen to the people around you, and to speak to them with humanness, your whole life will change. You'll find yourself bringing your skills not only to the podium, but to the negotiation table and the dinner table as well. You'll be credible under any circumstance.

The pros in any field make what they do look so easy. They run, kick, sing, dance, paint, and litigate seemingly without effort. But effort takes place behind the scenes. Speaking to audiences is easy too, when you've done the behind-the-scenes work. Is it a gift? Is it magic? If you make the commitment, you can make it look that way. Is it worth it? You decide.

VII

Sorcery Specialties

19

Special Speaking Situations

On the Telephone

Many people would rather speak on the telephone than face to face, because somehow they feel safer if they can't be seen. But from a communication standpoint, speaking on the telephone is actually more difficult because we're robbed of nonverbal feedback. Without visual cues, the entire conversation is dependent on the voice. Your voice, and your voice alone, puts the meaning into your message. It must convey to your listener that you're a warm, vibrant human being, and it must make the person on the other end of the line feel valued. While telecommunications technology makes the electronic connection possible, it's up to you, using your voice, to make the connection personal.

Some telephone experts advise people to speak slowly when they're on the phone so their words can be clearly understood. But studies show that without visual reinforcement, listeners quickly become bored, so when you're on the phone, you must speak with energy. Vocal energy, remember, comes from the diaphragm, so push down on the Plunger and get to the point.

Without visual reinforcement, vocal expression is more important than ever. Articulate clearly, making sure the endings of your words can be heard. Take advantage of your full vocal range, vary the volume, and make use of pauses to keep people listening. It helps to know that physical dynamism increases vocal dynamism. Even though your listeners can't see you, they will hear subtle changes in your voice if you sit up straight, put a smile on your face, and use your body when you speak. Some telecommunications trainers advise companies that rely heavily on telephone sales to put mirrors in their phone rooms, so their sales reps can check on their facial expression as they speak.

The absence of visual cues also increases the need for verbal feed-back from you. Since you can't see each other, it's important to lis-ten—really listen—to the other person. Periodically insert verbal fillers, such as "uh- huh," "yes," and "I see," to signal that you're alive and well and that you're following the conversation. It's also helpful to confirm what you think you hear by paraphrasing key points.

The Speech of Introduction

Every speaker deserves a good introduction, one that prepares the audience to welcome both speaker and subject. When you have the job of introducing a speaker, accept it as the key responsibility it is. Your role, though brief, can make a great difference to the success of the event.

Keep the introduction brief. State the speaker's name (one sen-tence), summarize his qualifications (four or five sentences), men-tion the topic (one sentence), touch on the topic's importance to the audience (a few sentences), and present the speaker. Say, "Ladies and gentlemen, I'm pleased to present to you Mr. Thomas K. Smith," or "Please welcome Mr. Tom Smith." Then look at Mr. Smith, smile, and start the applause. It's not necessary to say, "May I present..."

If you can insert a personal touch, by all means do so, but make sure everything you say is accurate. Check the speaker's credentials and make sure you pronounce his name correctly. At a recent con-ference, I had the honor of introducing the keynote speaker, who was also a personal friend. When I, in my best form, gave a personal anecdote designed to set him up with style, I made two critical, factu-al errors that he had to correct before he could get on with his address. It was not one of my better moments and could have been avoided if I had checked my facts with him beforehand.

Moderating a Panel

Moderating a panel can be a wonderful experience, but it requires a clear understanding of your role and a willingness to go out on a limb for the sake of good conversation.

As the moderator of a panel, you're more than a speaker. You're the coordinator and director of the discussion, making sure the panel knows exactly what's expected of them, the audience is comfortable, and that everything proceeds as planned. Without strong coordina-tion, panel speakers tend to go off into their own worlds, with the program becoming disjointed and hard to follow. It's your job to keep things running smoothly.

To ensure a successful panel discussion, it's a good idea to meet with the panel members ahead of time to acquaint them with each other and set the stage for a team effort. If a preliminary meeting is impossible, a telephone briefing with each one is a must. Impress upon them the importance of the throughline (the underlying theme of the program) and the desired objective (what you want the audience to do with the information they're providing). Remind them of time constraints and that it's death to any panel discussion when the speakers run overtime. Tell them your job is to keep the program running smoothly and that you will interrupt them if they speak past their allotted times. (Then be prepared to do it.) They will likely cooperate good naturedly with you if they know the ground rules ahead of time.

Your opening remarks provide you with an opportunity to set an energetic and upbeat tone. Tell the audience what the topic of discussion is and why it's important. Give them the throughline and let them know what you want them to leave with. The more you bind the pieces together at the beginning, the more interesting the event will be for everyone.

You can introduce all the panel members right up front or individually when the time comes for each to speak. If you've set the stage well, a few words as each speaker begins will suffice. Keep the introductions short, especially if the audience has been provided with written bios. Make sure you've familiarized yourself thoroughly with the credentials of each speaker, so your introductions are accurate and you can direct questions to the appropriate respondent.

Some panel discussions are organized so that one member speaks and fields questions, after which the second speaker takes a turn, followed by a third, and so on. This is really just a series of speeches and not a discussion at all. A much more interesting and lively event will ensue if you encourage the panel members to interact with each other, as well as to answer the questions that come from the floor.

Be prepared with questions of your own. As the "voice of the audience," you can ask the tough questions, ones that others may be hesitant to ask. You'll stimulate lively discussion and motivate audience members to join in.

Keep your eye on the time and be ready to call a halt in preparation for a prompt close. Allow a couple of minutes to summarize the main points of the discussion, remind the audience of the through-line and program objective, and thank the panel. If they've looked great and get all the credit, you've done your job well.

Giving a Team Presentation

There may come a time when you're not the star of your own show but part of an ensemble cast, one player in a team presenta-tion. A good team presentation has the potential to be a smash hit, with the sizes, shapes, and delivery styles of multiple speakers adding life to the performance. There are, however, inherent dangers in group presentations, since during your preparation and rehearsal period, you are working "by committee." You'll need to work togeth-er closely and orchestrate your performance with care.

Make the first meeting of the group a strategy session. Plan your presentation according to the guidelines laid down in Chapter 11. Analyze your audience together, spelling out their level of expertise, their "need to know," and their general receptiveness. Determine the throughline on which to hang the presentation and make sure every-one on the team is aware of and subscribes to the same objective. What you want this audience to do with the information you're giv-ing them must be crystal clear to all of you.

Now choose your chunks. Decide among yourselves what the main categories will be and what points are to be covered within those categories; then assign each chunk to a presenter. One member of the team should be assigned to open and close the presentation and to make sure the torch is passed gracefully from speaker to speaker.

Map out the visuals as if they are to be a part of one complete pre-sentation, which they are. I once coached a team presentation in which each presenter had been given a format for visual aids. There were to be four parts: objectives, staff, procedure, and results. By the time the seventh speaker had discussed the objectives, staff, proce-dure, and results for his particular section, I was ready to scream. We salvaged the presentation by eliminating much of the repetition, but weeks of preparation time was wasted in the process.

Conclude your first meeting by making sure all assignments are clear. If you can meet in person during this phase, great. If not, do it by telephone, fax, or video conference call, but do it. A good plan-ning session will assure that you're all working together, and your presentation will have a cohesiveness that will be evident to the audience.

Rehearsals should be just that—simulations of a real performance. It's one thing to sit around in a circle and talk about what you're going to say when you get up there. It's another to actually get up there and behave as if the audience were already in their seats, listening carefully to what you have to say. Treat each rehearsal like a dress rehearsal, with slide projectors and flip charts in place and in use. Practice handing off to the next presenter and asking each other tough questions during a simulated Q&A. Check for topic overlap and be ruthless in editing out redundancies.

Questions always arise about who should participate in a team presentation. You'll want to consider two criteria.

First, people who are closely tied to the project should be part of the team. If you're presenting to a client, the person with the greatest client contact needs to play a major role, perhaps as the team leader or moderator. More and more, technical specialists are being called upon to participate in sales presentations, since they know and understand the product and can provide necessary details about specifications, quality control, and delivery schedules. They've become an integral part of the sales team and should be included whenever possible.

Second, assign lengthy sections to the better presenters, or make sure all members of the team receive some training and coaching. A solid game plan can prop up and support a weak speaker, but there's no reason why he or she can't be quickly brought up to speed and helped to play an equal part in the proceedings.

Team presentations provide you the opportunity to experience ensemble performance. Like all ensembles, they require good direction and precision execution. And because the audience will respond to the team spirit you convey, they also require a sense of fun and adventure.

Impromptu Speaking

What if you don't have time to prepare? Not all the speaking we do is in a formal, stand-up mode. Much of the time we're caught unaware, brought in at the last minute for a project update, unexpectedly asked for our opinion. Some people become tongue-tied, not knowing where to begin. Others just start talking, figuring if they talk long enough, something significant will eventually occur to them.

Extemporaneous speaking is often a difficult communication skill to master. If you don't have the luxury of adequate preparation time, or if someone asks you unexpected questions and you need to answer immediately, there are formulas that will help you think on your feet. The one I like best is PREPO.

POINT. First, make your point. This is your major statement and should convey only one idea.

REASON. Next, give your reason for making that point. The reason answers the question, "Why do you say that?" It allows you to expand somewhat on your first statement. The reason you give is more specific than your point, but not so specific that it becomes...

EVIDENCE. Now provide supporting information. This is where you put data, demographics, and examples that back up and reinforce your point and reason. Evidence can be in "bullet" form, or might tell a story that illustrates the point you've made. Evidence should be specific; this is where the proof lies.

POINT. Now make your point again. Good evidence will lead you directly back to your main point. Use the same words, or better yet, rephrase your point, but it shouldn't change in content or attitude.

OBJECTIVE. This is a quick, action-oriented wrap-up. Use it to state an action for you, an action for your audience, or simply to balance and close your argument.

For example:

POINT: We need another salesperson on our staff.

REASON: The two people we have now are swamped with work.

EVIDENCE: Mary has all she can handle with existing accounts. John's time is spent on the phone taking incoming calls. Neither has time to drum up new business.

POINT: If we're going to grow, we need to add another salesperson to the staff.

OBJECTIVE: I've drawn up a plan and I'd like you to take a look at it.

Here's how this PREPO would look in narrative form. "We need another salesperson on our staff, because Mary and John are swamped with work. Mary has all she can handle with existing accounts, and John spends all his time on the phone taking inquiries.

Neither one can get out on the road where we need someone drumming up new business. If we're going to grow the way we want to, we've got to have someone else in sales. So I've drawn up a plan and I'd like you to take a look at it."

When you're called upon to speak "off the cuff," take a quick moment to breathe and center yourself. While you're doing that, think to yourself, "What's the point I want to make here?" And you're off and running.

In a seminar, I once gave this assignment: "Develop a PREPO statement on any subject that will take a minute or two to give. You have 30 seconds to prepare." As we went around the room and each attendee delivered a PREPO, I noticed that Bob, who was to be the last speaker, was thinking harder and harder. When his PREPO was completed successfully, I asked what he had been thinking about, and he made us all laugh by saying, "Well, someone gave my Prepo so I had to write another one. Then someone else gave that one. The one you heard was the third one I thought up." Bob's major speaking problem was that he was exceptionally long-winded, so creating three short, tight presentations in the space of ten minutes was a remarkable achievement for him and a giant step toward his becoming an impressive speaker.

PREPO gives you the confidence that you can think on your feet and compile brief, coherent remarks in a very limited amount of time. Work with PREPO like every other tool in this book. Practice it when you're alone, and when you find yourself under pressure, it will come naturally to you.

Special Problems of Men and Women

Throughout this book I've studiously avoided talking about what men "should do" or what women "should do" when they speak to groups. That's because I strongly believe there need be no significant difference. The techniques and exercises in this book are for everyone. The skills they develop help people become better presenters. Not just men, and not just women.

More and more the general public is coming to understand what researchers have known for a long time, that there is no such thing as inherently "masculine" behavior or "feminine" behavior. Instead, there are patterns of behavior that are perceived as strong and other patterns that are perceived as weak. The best way to become a good speaker is to practice those behaviors that add authority and conviction to your presentation, and to eliminate anything that weakens you or your message.

In the studio, we find that men and women tend to show their nervousness in different ways, even though the degree of nervousness is about the same for both. Women generally don't hesitate to admit their fear and often display it openly, while men go quickly into overcontrol, shutting down completely to defend themselves against vulnerability. Because so many men are prone to overcontrol, it's difficult for them to loosen up, move freely, and use gestures effectively. Instead of expressing themselves openly and naturally, they tend to pace back and forth, drift aimlessly about the platform, or rhythmically beat time to their words with their hands. But these are not "men's problems," they are expression problems.

Admittedly there are physical differences between men and women that can cause difficulties, but they can easily be overcome. In most cases women are smaller than men, so they need to adopt stronger postures and work harder to take command of their space. Because their voices lie in a higher range, their vocal problems are more grating to an audience. On the whole, women tend to experience dramatic improvement in the way they sound through the use of the Plunger, and their high-pitched, little-girl voices settle and deepen, increasing their credibility.

One reason I'm reluctant to offer advice in the form of hard and fast rules for each of the sexes is that it can backfire. Let me give you an example. There's a big difference between a hearty laugh of enjoyment and a high-pitched nervous giggle. Both men and women occasionally laugh from embarrassment, but because a woman's laugh has a higher pitch, the nervous giggle has come to be thought of as a "female" characteristic. A nervous giggle is awful to hear, so some women have been told that they shouldn't laugh in a business setting. This is a terrible piece of advice that makes no sense at all.

I've never heard of a man being told he's not supposed to laugh in business. Easy, relaxed response to humor goes hand in hand with poise and confidence, and confident professional people kid with each other and laugh together often. The solution to the problem of the nervous giggle, of course, is not to put a lid on yourself that stops you from laughing. It's to train yourself to respond vocally in an open and healthy manner that's not fraught with tension. The problem of a nervous giggle isn't a "women's problem." It, too, is a vocal problem.

The techniques and exercises in this book are for everyone. They're designed to help people become better presenters, and they work equally for men and women.

20

Managing the Difficult Audience

One friend, one person who is truly understanding, who takes the trouble to listen to us as we consider our problems, can change our whole outlook on the world.

—Elton Mayo

The single most devastating punishment that can be inflicted on any of us is being forced to be alone. I don't mean the "getting away from people" solitude we seek when we take off for a weekend in the mountains or choose a quiet evening at home over a university lecture on mid-eastern politics. The aloneness I'm talking about is that awful feeling of total physical and, even worse, emotional isolation from other human beings that's sometimes thrust upon us. We're out there with no one we can draw strength from, no one who will help us. We're abandoned, alienated from everyone who matters.

This dread of aloneness is the reason why so many speakers fear even the suggestion of facing a difficult audience. Suddenly the lines are drawn, and it's you against them. You're standing there isolated and vulnerable, your words defenseless against their scorn. Instead of talking with a group of people you can identify with, who have the same needs and feelings as you, it seems that you're a single warrior lined up against a regiment of bitter adversaries.

A difficult audience, or more accurately the difficult members of an audience, are those who experience feelings of denial or hostility toward you or your message. They're hurting, fearful, anxious people who have already judged what you're about to say and found it wanting. Usually they're looking for confirmation of their own viewpoints and will seize on anything in your words or delivery that will reinforce their convictions.

And here you are, all set to make a strong, positive, caring connection with people who don't seem the least bit interested in hearing your side of the story. No wonder even experienced speakers are unnerved. But like any other time you're involved in conflict, you have a challenging opportunity to turn the situation around and gain something positive from it for both you and your audience.

There are two types of difficult audiences, passive and hostile. To my mind, the more difficult is the passive audience where people don't respond. They don't laugh, they don't question, they don't argue, they just...sit. When I speak to a passive audience, I feel that I'm talking into a giant cotton ball that absorbs all my energy and gives nothing back. I always want to try harder and give more, but I've learned through bitter experience that this is a mistake. The more I try, the more they resist.

On the other hand, the audience we commonly think of as hostile is the highly-charged group whose emotions are on the surface and who are ready and willing to refute you—loudly and in full public view. Believe it or not, there's an upside to having an angry, emotionally-charged audience.

Because an emotional audience is an interested one, and you don't have to overcome boredom or passivity, they're paying attention from the moment you walk in the room.

Don't Get Defensive

When faced with an audience of disillusioned, disgruntled people, speakers often respond in ways that only make the situation worse. They argue with the audience or try to persuade them to change their minds by "thinking logically."

Speakers threaten, preach, order, advise, admonish, ignore, distract, blame, criticize, or impugn the motives of their listeners. Some speakers even manage to do all these things at once.

Even though engaging in one-upsmanship may temporarily give you a lift, it's never successful in winning over an audience. You must never forget your goal of establishing a connection between you, no matter how much of an effort it is in the beginning or how tough the audience makes it for you. Your unfailing respect for them in the face of continued hostility can change their perception of you and may even result in a more cooperative attitude on their part.

Try an experiment. Hold your hand up, palm out and fingers open. Ask someone to place his hand against yours so your palms and fingers are touching. Now push. Notice how, without thinking, your partner pushes back. This "push-push back" phenomenon is the basis for most of the problems evolving out of our interactions with others. Pushing back is our natural, instinctive response to pressure.

A difficult audience, be it hostile or passive, will push you to your limits. You absolutely, positively cannot afford the luxury of pushing back. So what can you do? Well, start by taking another look at where they're coming from.

Start From Where They Are

Your audience feels the way it feels, and simply wanting it to feel differently won't change a thing. So start from where they are by making sure your initial audience analysis gives you the best possible prediction of how receptive they're likely to be. You can then take some early steps to diffuse their negative feelings and lower their resistance.

You may want to change your objective to one less strong than the action-oriented objective I recommended in Chapter 11.

Instead of asking them to do something definitive in response to your remarks, it might be better to ask a difficult audience to "listen to your point of view," "weigh your arguments carefully against their own," or "reserve judgment until they've heard your story."

An effective technique used in sales presentations is to "handle the objections up front." Right at the beginning, the salesperson, knowing ahead of time that the customer is going to balk at the price, says something like, "This is an expensive gizmo, but after I've shown you how much better it works than the gizmo you have now, I'm sure you'll see that it's more than worth the money." Because the price question has been openly addressed, the customer doesn't have to worry about bringing it up, so she can relax and listen to the presentation.

One time I spoke to a group of school superintendents about making effective media presentations. This group had originally wanted a professor from a nearby university to work with them, but he was busy so I got the call. I opened my presentation by saying: "According to your standards, I'm not a 'real' teacher. I have absolutely no academic background in education. But I do share with you a love of helping people learn something they can use in their lives, and I look forward to sharing with you the results of my own work in the field of communication."

Later, when the superintendents were asked what I had said or done during the session that made me credible in their eyes, many of them answered, "You didn't try to fool us by pretending to be like us. You even made 'not being a teacher' a strong point." My comments were effective because I didn't wait for *them* to make the argument. I brought up the subject myself, got it out of the way, and carried on with the session.

Another great way to lower defensiveness in the audience is to give them permission to disagree with you. I call this, "asking for the 'yes buts'." Because I'm not a lawyer, attorneys tell me, "I'm sure you're right, but in my situation..." I hear from accountants, "Yes, but when I'm speaking to my clients..." Other people say, "That's all well and good, but..." Instead of pushing back and arguing that I'm the expert in speaking and communication and they're not, I ask for those comments. I tell them to call out their "yes buts" whenever they occur, so we can look at how my theory can be applied to their needs. What usually happens is that everyone good-naturedly looks for ways to stump me, we get into some great discussions, and everyone, including me, learns a lot more.

Change the Order of Your Presentation

In Chapter 11, I recommended that you lay out your speech for your audience in broad, general terms by clearly stating in your introduction exactly what you're going to talk about, your through-line, and your objective. You should then go back and fill in the chunks, adding detailed support that backs up and reinforces your main points. Your wind-up should include a summary of your main points, a repeat of your thesis statement, and a call to action. Structured like this, your presentation has a beginning, a middle, and an ending that takes you back to the beginning, closing the circle and giving you a sense of completion and closure.

When you're dealing with a difficult audience, especially a hostile one, this may be too strong. It's likely that they've already decided your premise is wrong, and if you start out by proclaiming it unequivocally, you'll turn them off completely. An alternative is to start from an area of common ground. Begin with a specific fact with which you can all agree. Perhaps neither side wants to see staff cuts or layoffs, so start by talking about that. Or describe your vision of a traffic-free, undisturbed neighborhood *before* you introduce the plans for improved traffic flow.

Once you've established a commonality of purpose, you can then build, step by step, through your argument, ending with the conclusions you want them to reach. This is a much softer approach to persuasion. You'll find beautiful examples of it in the parables of the Bible and in Aesop's Fables. If I quietly tell you about The Fox and the Grapes, by the time I'm finished, we both agree on the moral of the story. This way of structuring a presentation isn't guaranteed to sway everyone to your way of thinking, but it can greatly reduce people's fears and soothe a potentially volatile situation.

Learn to Listen

A key principle of interpersonal communication is that you must address the emotional issues of a situation before you can enter into a logical discussion. No one whose mind is in turmoil, or who is filled with anger, or fear, or suspicion, or despair will be able, let alone willing, to hear what you have to say.

Knowing how to listen will enable you to guide your audience to the point where they can focus on your message. It may be that you'll have to postpone your formal presentation and give them an opportunity to let off steam. Even if you start out unaware of how angry they are, once you realize it, put your original objectives on hold and spend your time listening.

Listening is the act of receiving and interpreting spoken messages, but there's much more to it. Listening means fully understanding the message you're hearing from the *other person's* point of view. Listening demands your active participation and is an integral part of the speaker-message-audience loop.

You accomplish it, not only with your ears, but with your eyes. When you watch the nonverbal behavior of the audience carefully, you'll pick up clues that go far beyond their spoken words. Your goal is to receive the whole message and feed it back to the audience so they feel heard and understood.

Being a good listener doesn't mean that you're obligated to cave in and agree with the other person. I'm not telling you it's okay when I say: "It's hard for you to rehearse your presentations adequately because there are so many urgent demands on your time." But by understanding how difficult it really is for you to practice, I can speak about repetition and practice in a way that has more relevance for you. Good listening reduces the need for rebuttal and argument and strengthens the connecting thread between speaker and audience.

Four Ways to Listen

There are four ways you can respond to the audience to let them know you're with them. First, you can paraphrase the content of their message and feed it back.

Paraphrasing is summarizing what the other person has said in your own words. When you're paraphrasing, you're not concerned with the feelings of the message. You're only communicating the facts as you think you've heard them. "You're saying that the depositions won't be ready on time, and we'll have to get the trial date postponed for another two weeks, is that right?" Message sent, message received, message acknowledged.

The second way to listen is to watch the nonverbal behavior of the audience and feed that back, regardless of the message they think they're sending. "You haven't asked me any questions, but I see a lot of puzzled looks out there. Am I confusing you?"

In the midst of a talk I was giving, I noticed that half the heads in the auditorium were nodding "yes" and the other half were nodding "no." "Some of you look skeptical," I commented. "Let me go back and make that point again and see if I can clarify it for you." I don't know that I converted anyone else to my point of view, but we had an enjoyable session together because I acknowledged the legitimacy of their feelings by responding to their silent messages.

Third, use your own nonverbal signals to encourage your audience to keep talking. Keep your posture open and relaxed, maintain good eye contact, and carefully avoid any defensive gestures or mannerisms. Gentle head nods, smiles (or frowns) of understanding, and small sounds like "uh huh," and "hmm" will keep the lines of communication open and, at the same time, keep the focus of attention on the sender.

The fourth way to listen, and the most difficult to master, is to reflect. This involves feeding back both the emotional and the factual parts of the message, with the most critical emphasis placed on the emotional content. To reflect, listen to the sender's entire message, including the feelings being expressed or just hinted at, and feed all of it back to that person in your own words. "I hear you saying that you're angry because you weren't consulted about the location of the new fire station. It's being put in your neighborhood, but you didn't have a voice in the decision."

Notice that I've neither agreed or disagreed with your position. I haven't tried to defend the city's decision to put the fire station in your neighborhood. I've only reflected back what you said, along with the emotion I heard behind the words.

At first it will feel strange to probe the sender's emotional state, especially if you're generally uncomfortable talking about feelings with business associates. But when emotions run high, they must be acknowledged and diffused *before* you can return to any meaningful message of your own.

Errors to Avoid in Reflection

Very few of us listen well. There's a great tendency to grab control of the conversation and turn it back to you and your presentation. Remember, listening is all about the *other guy*. You'll increase your chances for successful listening if you guard against these common mistakes.

Don't exaggerate or diminish their feelings. Don't say, "I can see how *furious* you are," when they're only mildly irritated. If you miss the degree of their feelings by too much, the impact of your reflection will be lost.

Don't add or omit information. "You're concerned about possible layoffs in this department, and you want to know about the restructuring plan"—okay so far—"and there have also been complaints about the puddles in the parking lot, but there's nothing we can do about that because it's not on the agenda." Now you've weakened your case. Make your reflection and quit while you're ahead.

Don't play shrink. It may be that your audience is blaming you for the slump in sales because you've just replaced a manager they liked and admired. However, it will only make matters worse if you throw it back in their face by accusing them of being resentful. Instead say something like, "It's tough to face up to the fact that the job isn't getting done. Let me see if I can put it in perspective." This way you've reflected the facts and the feeling, but left the motivation behind it to the psychologists.

Don't parrot (repeat the sender's words verbatim). If you hear, "Our union will not agree to a no-strike clause until we are assured of job security," don't say, "The impression I get is that your union won't agree to a no-strike clause until you're assured of job security." If you parrot the message, you won't sound anything like a caring, compassionate listener. You'll just sound like a parrot.

Don't say, "I know how you feel." The automatic response to that will be, "Like hell you do." If you reflect the content and the emotions of the message in your own words, you'll demonstrate your understanding, without having to proclaim it.

Above all, don't fake it. The biggest mistake you can make is to go through the motions of listening without really making the effort to put yourself in the other person's position. You'll not only come across as phony and insincere, you'll be phony and insincere. The listening part of speaking is as dependent on honesty and integrity as the speaking itself.

Talk About Yourself

A good way to get your own feelings across without confrontation when you're speaking to a difficult audience is by using the "I" statement technique. An "I" statement is one that emanates from you as a person rather than a statement made about somebody else. For example, if I say, "You're never around when I need you," I'm talking about you, and I sound as if I'm attacking you. You'll hear the attack, automatically push back, and pretty soon we'll be embroiled in a big argument. But if instead I use an "I" statement, "I miss having you here to talk to." I've only expressed how the situation seems to me. There's absolutely nothing to argue about, and there's a chance that you'll suggest, on your own, that we get together and talk.

A city council member began a talk at an angry neighborhood meeting with an "I" statement. "I feel like I'm walking into a lion's den this evening," she smiled. "And I only hope that, at the close of this meeting, you'll find you aren't quite as hungry for my flesh as you thought you were."

This speaker accomplished a lot with her opening. She expressed her own honest feelings about the situation, she gave the group permission to be critical of her, and her smile showed that she accepted them and wasn't threatened by their hostility.

Audience members, in the grip of their own emotions, don't always realize how their actions are affecting the speaker. In a positive, non-threatening way, "I" statements call attention to the problem, and audience behavior often changes dramatically in response to the speaker's frank and straightforward expression.

21

Meeting the Media

At some time, you may find yourself representing your organization at a press conference or media interview, called upon to answer questions about its actions, policies, products, personnel, or other matters. The interview may be for a magazine or newspaper article, or you may be invited to appear on a radio or television talk show, or a microphone may suddenly be thrust into your face and you find yourself prominently displayed on the six o'clock news.

When you meet the media, you are conversing with an interviewer, but you are really talking to your many publics—customers, shareholders, employees, competitors, creditors, or the Joneses next door. These are the people you want to win over, and your goal is to get them to listen to you, to like you, and to think positively about your company. The interviewer is only the conduit through which you send your message to the people who matter most.

Many business leaders labor under the misconception that reporters hold a negative bias toward business and don't understand the topics and industries they write about. It's easy to think of media people as "the enemy," but this is simply not the case. Of course, there are some reporters who sensationalize events, and some who are careless about how they present the facts, but journalism is a competitive field, and most reporters are competent professionals. Reporters assigned to business stories usually have a background in some aspect of business as well as journalism.

You can make the most of the opportunities the media offers by working with journalists and broadcasters rather than treating them as adversaries. If part of your job is to handle media relations, give it your personal attention and make it a high priority. Take some time to get to know the reporters and news executives who cover your industry, keep in touch with them whenever it's appropriate, and do your best to provide them with clear, factual information.

Before the Interview

Whether you're a harried spokesperson in the midst of a fast-breaking story or have plenty of lead time, it's vital that you take time out to plan a strategy that will carry you through the interview, or interviews, ahead. What is your position on this subject, and what support do you have for that position? Why is it important to talk about this? What are the main points you want to cover? Are there any popular misconceptions you need to clear up? What factors limit your ability to respond to questions on this subject? How much information can you disclose? What are the legal ramifications? And are there topics you can't discuss, no matter what the circumstances?

Give some thought to the makeup of your audience. Who is likely to be watching, or listening, or reading about you as a result of this interview? What are the fears they may have? Are there sensitive areas you should address? Is this controversial? Is anyone angry? Is your intent to interest and excite people, or calm them down and smooth things over?

Find out as much as you can about the interview itself. What is its purpose? Who is the interviewer? Does he or she have anything personal to gain from the exchange? Do you? Where will it take place? How much time will you have? Will anyone else be interviewed at the same time, and if so, will that person be in agreement with you or on the opposing side?

What questions are you most likely to be asked? Anticipate them and write them down, especially the tough ones you hope won't come up. Then write specific answers to each question. Familiarize yourself thoroughly with the answers so you are comfortable with them. Then practice speaking them in your own words. Don't memorize your answers or you'll tend to recite them mechanically.

The more you can anticipate and prepare for the interview, the more quickly you'll be able to think on your feet when your adrenaline is pumping and the microphone is on. You'll give a better interview if you eliminate as many surprises as possible.

During the Interview

The Sword of Damocles that hangs over the head of many a corporate spokesperson is the thought that an invesitgative reporter might show up on the doorstep at any moment. No matter who is coming to call, it's necessary that you treat your interviewer like a human being who has a job to do. Even if you're face to face with a tough questioner like Sam Donaldson or Mike Wallace, deal with the issues, not the interviewer's personality. Treat that person as a partner, helping him or her do a good job by supplying information willingly and courteously. Your efforts to be helpful against all odds will be evident to the public, and remember, they're the audience you're trying to reach.

When giving an interview:

1. Always be honest and tell the truth. Even if it hurts. Your integrity will heighten your own credibility and that of your organization. You can, however, neutralize negative information by putting it into perspective. You aren't obligated to answer a question just because it's put to you. If you can't give out certain information, decline to answer, and say why.

2. Stick to your own message. Use every opportunity to get the points across to the audience that you want to cover. If the questioning begins to pull you off the track, bridge back to the subject by saying something like: "That's not really the issue here. The point I'd like to make is...."

3. Say what you have to say quickly and concisely. Time is a major consideration. Pause for a moment, then answer the question right up front, elaborating only if time allows. Practice giving answers that are brief and to the point. You should be able to condense all pertinent information into a 20-second answer.

4. Speak through your interviewer. If you're appearing on TV, look at the interviewer, not at the studio audience or into the camera. Remember who your target audience is and speak through the interviewer to those people.

5. Speak to the undecided. There are three kinds of listeners: those who always agree with you, those who never agree with you, and all the rest. All the rest are those who are uninformed or who haven't yet formed an opinion. They're the important part of

your target audience—the ones you want to reach and persuade.

6. Speak to the level of understanding of your audience. Most public utterances reach a very large audience, and the bigger the group, the more basic your language must be. Avoid jargon and technical terms. In order to bring abstract ideas to life, give examples of real people in real life doing real things.

On the other hand:

7. Don't speculate, exaggerate, estimate, or play the expert. If you don't know the answer to a question, say, "I don't know the answer to that one, and it would be inappropriate for me to speculate." Decline absolutely to answer hypothetical questions. Stick to what you know.

8. Don't give personal opinions or let your own feelings show in your face. You are the voice of your company, and as such, it's your responsibility to speak only those words that have been agreed upon ahead of time within your organization. In this role, your personal opinions don't count, so keep them to yourself.

9. Don't get defensive. Keep your cool at all times. Maintain an open posture and stay relaxed. Be open, attentive, and friendly, no matter what.

10. Don't go off the record. You can't be absolutely sure you can trust your interviewer. And even if there is absolute trust between you, there are often misunderstandings as to exactly which comments are on the record and which are off. Remember, the interviewer's job is to get a good story, and a good story means good quotes. To expect the juiciest comments to be withheld is asking for trouble. There are even cases of people who speak on the record, have second thoughts, then call the reporter asking that certain remarks be eliminated. They're shocked when they're rebuffed by the reporter, who "was so nice the day before." *If you don't want it made public, don't say it.*

Watch the Pros

The best education you can get in handling media interviews is to watch how the pros do it. The Sunday morning political programs provide a stimulating and entertaining battleground for interviewers and government officials to challenge each other over the week's events. And while many of the politicians featured are more evasive than you should plan to be in similar circumstances, most of them do an excellent job of getting their message across to the American public in an intelligent, articulate way. They skillfully block and parry the toughest questions and gently diffuse the hostility that occasionally arises. And the masters of their craft do it with great humor and style.

You can have a lot of fun conducting critical analyses of political talk shows, and I encourage you to watch them and see for yourself who and what makes a good interview. Who seems to be forthcoming with answers and is always cooperative? Who enjoys returning a zinging statement with one of his own? Who gets defensive and loses her cool. Who do you like and why? Who do you dislike and why? Watch the interviewers to learn how they work. What kind of questions do they ask? Do they ask the same question over and over again, continuing to probe, even when no one wants to answer? When do they let up and go on to another subject?

Who honestly seems to want information, and who is trying to say, "gotcha!"? What do their nonverbal signals tell you? Who is relaxed and who is uptight? How do you know? How can you tell when someone begins to get defensive. Do they tend to shut down because they're afraid "something will slip"? What vocal expression do they use, and at what point does your attention begin to wander?

Local shows provide the same educational experience, but at a slightly different level. Often the interviewees won't be as experienced, and you can compare their skills not only with the people at the top but with your own. You'll learn a lot about what to do and what not to do when you find yourself face to face with an interviewer. As a result, when the time comes for you to engage in a media performance of your own, you'll be way ahead of the game.

22

Lights...Camera...Action!

Lights...Camera...Action! When you chose a career, you probably never dreamed that responding to these words might be a part of your job. But the line between business and show business is disappearing as video technology breaks down the barriers. You don't have to be a professional actor or media personality to find a script thrust into your hand and a TV camera looming in front of you, and when it happens, you'll find you need your performance skills more than ever.

Today, most large companies and professional service firms are, to some extent, in the video production business. Video-taped messages spread the corporate word quickly and efficiently to every office and every employee. Forward-thinking organizations are using videotape for major announcements, product information, financial results, human resource information, sales presentations, promotional packages, and training sessions. And because it's much more personal to use a company's own people than talent hired from outside, the chances are good that at some point you'll be called upon to appear in a corporate video.

Video production is expensive. Producing a quality 30-minute video can cost upwards of $30,000 and can take as long as two days to shoot—days that have been preceded by many hours of script writing and other preparation. This is a hefty investment, and if you're a featured player, the way you deliver your lines can make or break the project.

Making a video presentation is not at all the same as speaking to a live group. I don't mean that you can ignore everything we've talked about here, but many accomplished speakers have found that skill before a live audience does not always guarantee success on television. It's easy to be cowed by the imposing atmosphere of a professional studio—the cavernous rooms, the bright lights, the snaking cables and glaring cameras, the technicians running around being mysteriously technical. It's also intimidating to realize that all your worst features are soon to be recorded and put on view for everyone to see—over and over again.

The key to a successful on-camera performance is to become familiar with all the activities that lead up to and surround a video shoot. The more comfortable you feel during the production process, the easier it will be for you to conduct yourself in a competent, professional manner. No matter how good a speaker you are, if you take the project for granted and try to "wing it," you may be in for some trouble.

Take Control of the Script

Reading from a manuscript is one of the most difficult things for a performer to do, which is why I advise against it in almost every situation. But video is different. You'll be required to read from a prepared script and that is your biggest challenge—to make the written word sound as if you were speaking your thoughts for the first time to a personal friend. So make sure from the beginning that those words are easy for you to say out loud. Can you speak without stumbling? Are these words you would use in real life? If not, they should be rewritten. Try reading the following sentence out loud.

> "At this current point in time, we are developing industry-specific and customer-specific operational programs, which will be supported through more competitive analyses, better market research, and increased proposal support, because these expanded operational capabilities will eventually produce correct, timely, and dependable systems that will be integral to this company's profitability and growth."

That sentence was taken directly from a business video script and was almost the downfall of an otherwise capable speaker. If you're given lines like these, change them. Go off somewhere, speak the ideas in your own words and write them down. Then give your notes and the script back to the writers with instructions to finalize it in *your* language. A good script will make you look good, so don't take any chances with it. But make sure the changes are made before the shoot. Studio time is expensive, and you don't want to use it up making script changes that should have been taken care of earlier.

Stay Relaxed

Even if you're relatively relaxed before a live audience, a taping session can be stressful. One way to avoid stress buildup is to go with the production flow. It helps to know that retakes are a part of the business, and even the most experienced actors often have to shoot a scene several times. Don't expect to get your performance right the first time, and don't get down on yourself if you lose your place or stumble over your lines. Everyone makes bloopers and they can be very funny, so if you make one, have a good laugh, shake it off, and then go back and fix it.

One of your toughest problems will be waiting for someone else to do his or her job. The technical work between takes can seem endless, but if you allow yourself to get impatient, you'll soon be exhausted. The more detached you stay from everyone else's activities, the more energy you'll have for your own work, and the fresher you'll be during the shoot's closing moments.

If you feel yourself tightening up, shrug your shoulders and take a few deep breaths. Be on the lookout for tension in your neck, jaw, and shoulder muscles, and shake it out. You don't have to feel self-conscious about doing relaxation exercises in front of the crew members. They've seen many a professional performer working to eliminate muscle tension and, besides, they're too busy to care.

Focus On Real People

Never forget that you're not just saying words, you're talking about real ideas to real people. This isn't easy to remember when you're eyeball to eyeball with a camera lens. Added to that, you'll only be looking at a small part of your script at a time—the dozen or so words that you'll be expected to say at that one moment. The teleprompter that displays these words is located directly in front of the camera, which "looks" right through it and films you while you're speaking.

When you look at the teleprompter, pretend that you can see right through it to the people who will be watching the tape. Talk directly to them. Picture them in your mind. How many of them are there? What are they wearing? Are they sitting in rows of chairs, behind their desks, or cross-legged on the floor? Is your mother there?

Real people are out there. Think of every one of them as your friend. When you speak only words, your eyes will look lifeless. But when you are talking about important ideas to friends, your eyes will come alive and sparkle with an enthusiasm that will be picked up by the camera.

Keep It Natural

Your natural gestures and mannerisms will work well for you during a video performance, especially if you've mastered the movement techniques contained in Chapters 9 and 10.

If you normally use your hands to make a point, do the same thing here too. Expansive gestures should be toned down a bit, though, since the camera's eye will tend to exaggerate them. It's usually better to gesture with one hand rather than two, because asymmetrical gestures look more graceful. Just as in every other speaking situation, avoid rhythmic patterns that make you look like you're beating time to your words.

Subtle body movements are quickly picked up by the camera and you can use them to convey special meaning. A shrug of your shoulder or a raised eyebrow will tell people a lot about what you're thinking. A tiny shift in the way you sit or stand can signal a new thought or a change of idea. Because the camera "sees" everything, nervous mannerisms like tapping your foot or playing with your wedding ring are very noticeable. That's why it's especially important that you stay relaxed and centered throughout your performance.

Learn to Walk and Talk at the Same Time

At some time during your performance, you may be required to move from one place on the set to another. In real life, this isn't hard to do. You're perfectly capable of getting up to close a window without interrupting a conversation. It gets more complicated when you must move on a certain cue to a designated spot so that your body is facing a certain way, while at the same time you're watching the teleprompter, thinking about the people behind it, and saying all the right words.

If your script includes movement cues, practice them beforehand. Get up from your chair and walk to the window while you read a particular line. Then repeat the move, speaking the line without reading it, so you can see where you're going. You'll soon learn that you don't have to glue your eyes to the prompter. In real life, you're expected to watch where you're going. It's perfectly acceptable to do the same when you walk on cue.

It's also a good idea to practice turning naturally. Some people stiffen up on camera and turn as if they were on a revolving stage, with their head, shoulders, and body all moving at exactly the same rate. How do you turn? Do you turn your head first and let your body follow? Or do your feet move first? It doesn't matter, as long as you're loose enough to do it that way on camera.

Dress For the Camera

Don't wait till the morning of the shoot to decide what to wear. Plan your wardrobe in advance. Suits in medium dark shades with pastel-colored shirts work well. Don't wear a white shirt or blouse, narrow stripes, or high contrast colors. Stick to solids or very subtle patterns. If a woman looks good in bright colors, it's fine to wear those colors on television.

Much has been said about the ever-present red tie on the performance-minded politician or executive. But a rich looking tie, especially a red one, is very attractive. Avoid seasonal fabrics, such as heavy wools or wrinkly linen, and anything highly trendy. And stay away from patterned socks and patterned or colored panty hose.

Be sure to wear comfortable shoes that are easy to walk in. Standing all day under hot lights can lead to swollen feet, and if your toes are pinched it will show in your face. Make sure everything fits well. Bring along your shaver, hair spray, and other toiletries you normally use. You'll have to refresh yourself numerous times during an all-day shoot.

It may be necessary for you to wear makeup. The bright lights will wash out even the strongest features, so makeup is an important part of dressing for the camera. Men, and even women unaccustomed to wearing heavy makeup, may find this disconcerting, but it's important to trust the judgment of the video production professionals with whom you're working. They'll make certain that you look your best. Remember that makeup is used routinely by other performers— media personalities, politicians on the talk shows, and all stage and screen actors.

Enjoy the Experience

If you've done your homework, you'll find that as you get into the project, video performance is fun. While in most presentations, you're all alone up there, here you're working as part of a talented, highly skilled team. Performer, producer, floor director, script writer, makeup artist, lighting technicians, camera crew, editor, and many others are all in it together.

There's something glamorous about being part of the world of electronic communication. And television (video production included) is the premier player in the industry. Because you're seen by more people than when you give a live presentation, you're likely to become something of a celebrity. The praise of colleagues and the glowing feeling that comes with a job well done are heady stuff indeed.

So, despite the "strangeness" of video performance to newcomers to the field, it has inherent rewards. You'll feel great satisfaction from your involvement. Familiarity with the process, preparation, and practice takes some preliminary effort, but the payoff at the shoot itself is more than worth it.

About the Author

Carolyn Dickson is founder and president of VOICE-PRO, Incorporated, a leading business communication consulting firm headquartered in Cleveland, Ohio. A dynamic business leader who herself once trembled at the thought of public speaking, Carolyn is now a sought-after speaker who has coached thousands of business professionals, including top corporate CEOs, from leading firms across the country.

Paula DePasquale is a Cleveland-area freelance writer and public relations professional.

To order additional copies of *Speaking Magic,* or to arrange for a speech or presentation by Carolyn Dickson, or to receive further information about the programs and services of Voice-Pro, please contact:

VOICE-PRO, Incorporated
2055 Lee Road
Cleveland, Ohio 44118

Phone: 216-932-8040
Fax: 216-932-5048

Index

visualization, use of, (see Rehersal, Mental)
vitality, appearance of, 65, 67
vital capacity, 51
vocal clarity, viii, 55
vocal harshness (see stridency)
vocal problems, vii, ix, 29, 52-53, 146
vocal signature, 47

vocal instrument, vii, 48-52
voice, active, 96-97
voice, passive, vii, 96
volume, 48-49, 102,
vowels, pronouncing, 56-57
windbag, the (exercise), 49-51, 134
words, choosing, 95-98
words, value-laden, viii, 97-98